12/5/08

To: Dr Taylor

Mike is a great program! Thanks for allowing me the opportunity to speak to the group.

# KEEP
# *SWINGING*

An Entrepreneur's Story of
Overcoming Adversity & Achieving
Small Business Success

## Jay Myers with Darren Dahl

NEW YORK

# Keep Swinging

Paperback ISBN: 978-1-60037-257-5
Hardcover ISBN: 978-1-60037-258-2

## Published by:

**MORGAN · JAMES**

THE ENTREPRENEURIAL PUBLISHER

www.morganjamespublishing.com

1225 Franklin Avenue Suite 325
Garden City, NY 11530-1693
800-485-4943
www.MorganJamesPublishing.com

**Habitat for Humanity**®
Peninsula
Building Partner

Cover design by:
Heather Kirk
Heather@GraphicsByHeather.com
Interior Design By:
Bill James
Bill@WAJames.com

Printed in the United States of America

# DEDICATIONS

I would like to dedicate this book to my late parents Dorothy and Jerry Myers, who taught me the value of honesty, integrity and ethics not only in business but in my personal life as well. Mom and Dad, I try to honor your memory everyday and run ISI in a way that would make both of you proud. Mom, you would also be proud that after all these years of working I still listen to you and have "my head down and tail up" and so do my employees. It's what drives all of us.

To my late brother John Myers, who was always my "answer man" and who taught me so much about business and life. The success of ISI is in tribute to you and all the words of wisdom and encouragement you provided me for so many years.

To my late brother Charlie, who never got a chance to see me grow up and make something out of myself. I still think about you often and what might have been.

To my late friend Ken Forbes, who early on encouraged me to get creative in recruiting for ISI and recommended to me to "hire the hustle." Ken, I took your advice and I think you'd be proud how it's all turned out.

# Keep *Swinging*

To my late friend Alan Salomon, my friend for over 14 years at ATS and ISI and who was the first to encourage me to write this book. Alan, I miss you and think you would like what we have put together.

To Dolores, Chris, Susie, my late brother John's wife Diane, Molly, Mike and Beth and all of my family who have been in my corner from the start. Thank you for believing in me and providing steady encouragement in good times and bad through the years. It's really meant a lot.

To all of the ISI employees, customers, partners, associates and friends of the firm, you folks are the best and thank you again for allowing me to start and grow ISI and to live out my dream. I could not have done it without you.

And finally to my wife Maureen, son Jordan and daughter Katie. None of what I have accomplished at ISI would have been possible without your love and support. You are the reason I do what I do and I love all of you very much.

# CONTENTS

# Keep *Swinging*

# Chapter One

# THE COURTROOM
*Remembering the Day My Business Almost Died*

I'm sitting in a Memphis courtroom on a damp and dreary November morning, first-row bench seat, holding my wife's hand. We're waiting for the judge, the Honorable Bernice Donald, to call the room to order. I'm squeezing Maureen's hand tight, too tight, but I can't calm myself otherwise. Today is sentencing day for Linda Merritt, the woman who almost single-handedly killed my company, Interactive Solutions. I've been waiting too long for this day, waiting for some kind of redemption, some kind of closure.

In a few minutes, I know I'll be called to testify in front of the judge, to retell the story that has plagued my dreams and has been my waking nightmare for 18 months. I will tell how Linda, formerly ISI's finance and accounting manager, pushed the business that I had been building for eight years to the brink of bankruptcy. She had stolen more than $257,000 from the company, from me and my employees, at a time when I was vulnerable, out of touch with the business after my brother unexpectedly passed away. I have been trying to forget that time, to move past her treachery, possibly even to forgive her. But the anger remains and it is hot.

I

# Keep *Swinging*

Sitting on that bench, I think back to the challenges I've overcome, the decisions I've made to grow my company into a thriving, $10 million-a-year business that's made the Inc. 500 list of the country's fastest growing companies two times. I think about my decision to walk away from my corporate career, to take the plunge in starting something new. I think about my partner, the guy I started the company with, and my decision to buy him out and tackle this on my own. I think about how my company provides directly for 16 families and that the long-distance video conferencing technology we install in schools and hospitals educates children and saves lives. I think about all the personal hurdles I've struggled through since going into business, surviving not only melanoma but also the deaths of my father, my mother and older brother. I think again about how Linda almost destroyed the one thing aside from my family that meant anything to me.

The Federal Prosecutor, Tracy Berry, who sits at a table in front of me turns around and nods. "You ready?" she asks. "I think so", I say, my voice cracking. I turn around to scan the mostly empty courtroom, wishing that all of my employees could have joined us, really wanting to acknowledge them. But the trial had been postponed several times so we could never plan to have everyone attend: we had a business to run. I received a phone call just this morning telling us to report, so Maureen was representing everyone who couldn't be here. "They are part of why I'm here," I say to myself, they're working to keep the business running

2

# The Courtroom

while I am here. This woman put all our lives at risk. If I don't convince this judge, she might go free. I know I need to do this - I need to relive the past and tell everyone what she did.

But I haven't seen Linda in almost a year and I wonder how I'll react to seeing her. We wait and I think back some more about the events that had led us to be sitting here. We wait and I squeeze Maureen's hand harder.

Then, BANG, everybody spins around to see a wheelchair-bound Linda rolling down the aisle, escorted by a bailiff, after crashing through the double-doors at the back of the room. She always knew how to make an entrance.

Seeing her, confined in her wheelchair, I can't help but feel a shred of pity. She looks small and harmless in her orange prison jumpsuit, a far cry from the fancy suits and jewelry I knew from before, before I helped send her to jail. Her hair, always so perfectly coiffed, is now greasy and matted. Her skin, which she had so often pampered with visits to beauty salons, now is ghostly pale and blotchy. She just doesn't look like the polished and cold-hearted thief I know she is. Will I be able to convince the judge to punish her for her past when she is clearly suffering now?

As the judge begins the proceedings, it is clear that Linda's lawyer, a court-appointed public defender, is out of her league. Standing before the judge, she tries to mount a defense, claiming her client, Linda, was a victim of identity theft - that she was innocent of the charges of bank fraud being brought against her. Tracy, on a counterattack, tears into Linda's past, her history of taking advantage of other business owners, her utter lack of concern for other human beings. Tracy is calm, but edgy. Her words cut. I see Linda wince more than once.

Then it's my turn. Tracy asks me to take the stand as a witness. Standing with my hand on the Bible, I look out at my wife, the people in the gallery and then Linda. When I look at her, she glances down at the floor, and I remember. I remember that day like it was yesterday. The day my business almost died.

*April 29, 2003*

The more I dig into the pile of paper on my desk, the hotter and redder my face gets. My shirt is soaked through with sweat. My hands are shaking. I'm frantic. I pound my computer monitor blaming it for printing the numbers I see on the screen. I feel like I've been kicked in the stomach. Goosebumps cover my skin. I have never been so scared in my life.

What am I supposed to do now?

I'm sitting in my office, on the outskirts of Memphis, Tennessee. My door is closed. I need to get a hold of myself, get a grip. I stand up and pace

# The Courtroom

around, my head spinning, trying to wake myself out of the nightmare I just waded into. The payroll numbers I'm looking at don't lie. Linda Merritt, my finance manager, had stolen from me, is probably still stealing from me. My receptionist appears to be in on it as well. But how much have they taken? My jaw is clenched so tight I can feel my molars buckle. As far as I can tell, so far thousands, tens of thousands, maybe hundreds of thousands of dollars worth of bogus bonuses and commissions dating back to July 2002 – almost to the day that my older brother died.

I look over at the pictures I have lined up on my desk. Maureen, my wife. Jordan and Katie, my children. My brother, John. When I lost him that summer, I mentally checked out of my business for a long time. He was my mentor, my big brother - my best friend. When our oldest brother Charlie died in a car wreck back in 1973, I leaned on John. When our dad died in 1999, there was John and his broad shoulders. He was always my go-to guy. Losing him disoriented me, left me questioning where I was headed with my life. I needed some time away from my business, time to pull myself together. I've been sleepwalking now for months.

I think back further, to 1996 when I started my business, Interactive Solutions. I gambled everything I had. I gambled everything my family had. I had been fired from my director level job with ATS, a well-respected local telecom company, and I wanted the chance to make something on my own. We had moved back to Memphis several years ago from North Carolina to get my career back on track. I had done the big company corporate thing for several years and decided to try a different route going to work for this smaller Memphis based telecom/data company. In a period of five short years, I built a video conferencing division from the ground up to a $5 million business unit within the company and in that time developed a real love for the technology. It was one of the main reasons why I decided to go out on my own. I wanted to leverage the last five years of my business life and create my own company that would sell video conferencing and audio-visual systems that could be used for everything from corporate meetings to creating virtual classrooms for rural school kids. My TV monitors, cameras and video technology are even being used to connect big-city doctors with remote hospitals. My business saves lives and I'm proud of it - proud of my 16 employees. We worked our tails off to become what we are today. Could it all be ruined now because I took my eye off the ball? Is all of this my fault?

When I took time off to mourn John, I counted on employees like Linda to keep things running smoothly at the office. I interviewed her, hand picked her, trusted her. Now, as I was discovering, she started stealing from me in my darkest hour. She was continuing to steal from me. I gave her keys to the books and the bank statements, even after I caught her using the company credit card to pay off her personal cell phone bill. How could I have been so stupid? I'm a numbers nut. I usually review everything. I deposit 99 percent of the company's checks. Why didn't I see this happening before now?

# The Courtroom

My God, I remember, Linda was at the funeral. I had just hired her. She said she had come to show her support. I had thanked her for coming. She was probably already plotting against us. My anger boils. I, we, didn't deserve to be betrayed like this. What am I going to do now? No question I'm awake now. I need answers.

I open my door and start barking out orders to my staff. As they gather and huddle in the kitchen near my office, they know something is wrong, but I don't have time to explain. Linda is out of the office with a broken ankle and I need information. Now! "Bring me the bank records," I say. "Where are the company credit card receipts? Get the payroll company on the phone. Hello. "Who authorized these bonuses?" I ask, "My finance manager? Don't you know she needs to get authorization from her boss? Yeah, me." "Oh my God," she says. "We didn't know." I slam the phone down.

It was dumb luck that I read an article in Inc. magazine last night, the May 2003 issue with Jennifer Lopez on the cover. In bed, while Maureen read her romance novel, I read about how brothers, Lloyd and Jim Graff, co-owners of Graff-Pinkert, a machinery supplier in Oak Forest, Illinois, uncovered an embezzler at their company. Seems that their bookkeeper, who had worked for the brothers for 11 years, had not only used the company charge accounts to buy toys and a backyard storage shed for herself, she had funneled more than $200,000 of the company's money into her personal accounts. Turns out she had a gambling problem. She just about bankrupted them, but they never suspected anything until it was almost too late. The only reason they uncovered her scam was because, when she went on vacation, she had forgotten to deposit the paycheck for Jim Graff, who served as president and treasurer, before she left. As Graff dug into the system to fix what he thought was just an oversight, he opened a Pandora's Box of problems: the woman had apparently been stealing from the company for more than four years. To make matters worse, they didn't have any insurance to cover the loss. In the end, they prosecuted her and, by tapping her company-sponsored profit-sharing plan, they were able to recoup about half their losses. The woman, who spent two years in jail, continues to send between $25 and $100 a month towards repaying the rest.

As I read the story, something clicked - that could happen to me. The image of the Graff's bookkeeper haunted me, lurking throughout the night, pushing me to check the books first thing in the morning. So I did. Thank God, the similarities between what Linda had done and what had happened to the Graffs was downright frightening. But what could I do now? What were my options? This was humiliating, a potential disaster if my employees found out. It might sink the company. What about my clients and vendors? Could I afford to confront this head on in public like the Graffs had? Could I afford not to?

# The Courtroom

I'm used to making decisions. Fast. I've never been very patient, I'm hyper and I wear my emotions on my sleeve. I'm also a man of faith and I've never raised my hand to my own children. But I've never shied away from a fight and I am not about to now. The stakes are just too high: my employees, their families, my family and my soul. I have given everything to this business and now this woman wants to take it away. I won't let her. So I do what I do best. I act.

After letting Maureen know that something was wrong, I call the local police in Germantown to report the theft. "A car will be right over," they say. Next, I want answers from my accounting firm. They had completed a full-blown audit just a few months earlier. I paid them thousands of dollars to go through my books with a fine-toothed comb, to modernize our computer system to prevent exactly this kind of problem. This wasn't a review or compilation – even if it wasn't designed to detect theft, they should have seen something was out of whack. To make matters worse, they were the ones that recommended Linda to me. They were the ones that told me, after watching her work with ISI and me over several months, that she sees the big picture. When I finally get them on the phone, I'm practically stuttering I'm so furious. "Why didn't you catch this?" I ask. "We'll look into it", they say. "Damn right you will." Slam.

# Keep *Swinging*

By now, Maureen is at the office and John DeLockery, my head of operations, joins us in my office. I'm pacing around, trying to come up with a plan. Maureen agrees to head over to the bank, to get them to dig up the cancelled checks and check the signatures on them. As she heads out, John says to me, "I think we know someone who can help. Remember Andy Wilson? We met him on a few trips with the Boy Scouts." "I do remember Andy," I say. "But I had no idea what he did." In the scouts, the adults don't usually talk shop. "Yeah I know," John says. "We got a chance to talk on a long drive back from one of our camping trips. He told me he was a forensic accountant and it sounded like this was the kind of stuff he usually dealt with." I didn't need any more prompting than that. "Great, what's his number?" I ask. John was right: Andy Wilson is a certified fraud examiner and forensic accountant and runs a business based in East Memphis. Forensic accounting is a profession similar to CSI, that television show. I want him to recreate the crime scene using numbers as the evidence to find wherever Linda's sticky fingers might have touched. "Andy, I need your help untangling this web," I plead on the phone. Turns out he knows about Linda – he's had to clean up after her before at another company, a local lumber company that she stole more than $2 million from. He's concerned that I called the police, though, "that was probably a mistake," he told me. It only created a lot of anxiety in the office and the cops couldn't do much. We still didn't have a handle on the whole situation and know Linda

# The Courtroom

might be tipped off that I was on to her. I felt sick: it was just a knee-jerk reaction. "Don't worry about it," Andy tells me. "I'll be over in the morning – just don't touch anything." Or anyone, I think. Linda is lucky she's out sick with a broken foot or something.

The receptionist, Angela Bell, isn't so lucky. The police question her to get a statement. Normally, she's bubbly and overly caffeinated. Now, she's different, stiff. She acts like she's been through this before, like she's reading off cue cards. What was her connection to Linda though? I remember that the previous summer I had asked Linda to hire a receptionist for us in the summer of 2002. I had no desire to deal with those issues after John died. Thinking back on it, I had no involvement in hiring Angela and spent very little time with her. But Linda certainly did. Come to think of it, they did spend an awful lot of time huddled together, often behind a closed door. Then there was that annual kickoff meeting which was held at the casinos in Mississippi – a company-subsidized business trip to Tunica. After we wrapped up meetings during the day, we would all head down and have some fun and I remember the two of them bragging about how much money they blew playing Black Jack and the slots together. I think back on a simple task that I asked Linda to do- hire a receptionist, to take care of it. She did all right. I try calling Linda, to get some confirmation about what had happened, but she isn't returning our phone calls. I fire Angela on the spot – we have enough proof of her involvement. (Little did I know how much she was involved – more on that later) Andy tells me I can't do that with Linda, we've got to be a little more gingerly about this- employment laws are funny and they mostly protect the employees. I can't just fire her without more evidence. But I'm thinking this woman stole from me. While I want to do far worse, I take Andy's advice and actually send some flowers to her house with wishes of a speedy recovery from her foot injury and asking her to check in with us as soon as she can. I wonder when is this nightmare going to end?

I head home, late. I am the last one to leave, locking the door to a dark and abandoned office. I wonder, is this a sign of things to come? I feel like hell, probably look like it too. I live only a few minutes away, but I drive around in circles, trying to come to grips with what happened today. I turn up the volume on the stereo, hoping for some relief by listening to my favorite Steely Dan guitar riffs. I wonder what my employees were thinking as they drove home. Are they now at home with their spouses, their children, wondering if they'll have a job tomorrow? Are they driving around like me or hunched over a pint of cheap beer instead? I'm tempted to go join them.

Today feels like a test of sorts, a day of reckoning. I think again about the stakes: this isn't just my life anymore; I'm working for 16 employee's families plus my own. Do I have what it takes to overcome and persevere – to save the business? I pull into my driveway and I see Maureen

# The Courtroom

in the doorway. I get out of the car and trudge up the path and into her arms. We'll get through this, she says. She has a way of smiling at me, a look that says - we can do this. Like always, I believe her. We will.

I've had some tough days running my business, but I'm still not sure how I made it through that day without snapping – the day I found out that Linda had lied to me, had stolen from me. I can't stop thinking that if I hadn't read that magazine article two nights ago…how long might this have continued to go on? I didn't sleep for the second night in a row, lying next to Maureen, staring at the ceiling and dreading what I would uncover the next day. I already found more than $40,000 missing in just 10 minutes. How much more was there? How much more could my business afford to lose?

At times, I wish the tale behind the starting of my business were a piece of fiction. Keep Swinging, however, is a true story filled with enough twists and turns to cause even John Grisham's eyebrows to perk up. That day in a Memphis courtroom was a judgment day of sorts for me and I am glad to be here today to tell you about how my business and I survived it. Now I am not Bill Gates or Howard Schultz, business superstars who can talk about how they launched billion-dollar empires. My story is one of a regular guy with a big dream who had to leap quite a few hurdles to build the business and the life I have today. The statistics vary, but most of the 600,000 businesses that are founded each year fail for a variety of reasons. Michael E. Gerber, author of E-Myth (Harper Business 1988), says four of five businesses fail before their fifth year. Even worse, only 4 percent of companies ever make it to their tenth anniversary. Many fall prey to a lack of capital, others from a range of maladies that includes partnership disputes and embezzlement. The rest, it seems, just run into some lousy luck. When I look back on the 11-year history of my business, Interactive Solutions in Memphis, Tennessee, I realize that we survived all of the traps above - and managed to invent some new wrinkles of our own.

Too often, I think, business books tend to just celebrate the success of a company after the fact or to try to make CEOs like Jack Welch into celebrities. Running a multi-billion dollar empire, however, brings far different challenges than starting your own company from scratch – which is what the majority of the 6 million small businesses in the U.S have done. The truth is that when you start a business, you're going to run into problems and too many business books focus only on the victories and not enough about what was learned through the defeats. That is why I feel like my story is one that will resonate with any prospective entrepreneur. Starting a business is easy. Starting and growing a successful business: not so much. While the chances of building the next Microsoft remain slim, the opportunity remains to build a sustainable business that can provide a living and healthy lifestyle not only for you

# The Courtroom

the entrepreneur, but for your employees as well. That is why I have written this trail guide of sorts to help prospective entrepreneurs avoid the missteps that have claimed so many others.

In just over 11 years, I have built a small business that, through its sales and installations of high-tech video conferencing and audio-visual equipment, now provides for more than 40 families. When we got started though, few people, especially in the Memphis area, had ever heard of video conferencing. It was our job at ISI to not only cultivate the relationships with companies, universities and hospitals to show them the possibilities of remote office communication, distance learning and telemedicine – but also to learn from the vendors the kinds of equipment and technical solutions that were available. That meant our customers paid us for figuring out what they wanted, like a high-tech conference room or a wired classroom complete with camera and microphones, then find the vendor who made the best equipment to fit that need (many of whom operated in Europe and around the world) and, finally, figure out how to install and service that final solution – not always an easy task. And as we have seen our customer's needs evolve over time, we have followed along, moving into the competitive audio-visual supply business, delivering things like digital signage and video walls, as well as developing customized software and hardware to meet specific needs like those of a dermatologist in Memphis trying to diagnose a case of skin cancer in a patient 200 miles away. In other words,

# Keep *Swinging*

ISI has evolved from a single-trick startup struggling to survive to a multi-million dollar a year company with installations in 40 U.S. States and 15 international sites. Notable clients include FedEx, Nissan, Oakridge National Labs, Ft. Knox, Bancorp South, and the University of Tennessee. We've also evolved physically, moving from a single executive suite, to an office in a strip mall on Highway 72 in Collierville to our current location in the Forest Hill Technology Park. In addition the company has a satellite office in Nashville, with field offices in Knoxville, Tenn. Birmingham, Ala. and Jackson, Miss. We're up to 40 employees as of the writing of this book and we've got plans to add a whole lot more. We've grown so much, in fact, that Maureen tells me she doesn't know all our employees by their first name anymore. At one time, the entire company could fit inside a single limousine.

Getting from point A to point B, however, wasn't easy. Facing cash flow problems, a partnership divorce and even an embezzling employee, there were many days when I thought my employees and I were going to end up as another startup casualty, just another statistic. We did in a way: we grew our company into one of a select few that have made the Inc. 500 – Inc. magazine's list of the fastest-growing private companies in America – more than once. Here is the story of how we did it, warts and all.

# The Courtroom

*Just Another Statistic – ISI makes the Inc. 500 list for the Second Time (2003).*

# Chapter Two

# GETTING FIRED

*The motivation to start a business*

Early on in my career, I learned something important about myself: I just wasn't suited for the corporate world. I always knew I wanted to run something of my own, so I focused on learning how to sell as soon as I graduated from the University of Memphis in 1978. With my business degree in hand, I could have done what most of my friends did and pursued a management or marketing type position with big companies that were recruiting me like Scott Paper or Procter & Gamble. But I was 22 years old and full of gumption and I didn't want to settle for any old job – I wanted the freedom of a sales job and I wanted the chance to earn some real money. So I passed on the big corporations and chose AM International instead: a rather large company with about $700 million in sales headquartered just outside of Chicago that manufactured printing equipment. They didn't offer me much - a sales job working on just about 100 percent straight commission. But I leaped at the chance. Maybe I wouldn't have a cushy salary to fall back on, but I only saw the unlimited potential to make money. This idea tapped something deep in me – turns out, early on; there were a few seeds of entrepreneurship in my soul. In other words, I wasn't afraid to take a huge risk and I had something to prove.

# Keep *Swinging*

And sales suited me. With some help from a few mentors, I was very successful with AM right away. I busted it right from day one. To be honest, I wasn't smart enough to do it any other way. In fact, I won a bunch of awards in the four years I worked there. I remember coming back to the office one day after spending the day making sales calls. I leaned back in my chair and put my feet up on an old gray metal desk I shared with another salesman, an older guy who had been around the block. After taking a look at me, he started to laugh: he saw that I had worn two holes right through the soles of my shoes. "Are you that cheap that you won't buy new shoes?" he asked me. "Nope, just haven't had time to go shopping," I said, pulling out the pieces of cardboard I had stuck in my shoes to keep the dirt out. And putting all that shoe leather to the pavement was paying off: By the end of my second year, I had pocketed about $37,000, which meant that I was already making more than my dad did. It was my boss at the time, however, that gave me one of the most memorable gifts I have ever received. As you can imagine, at 22 years old, outside of working hard, my priorities were more about looking cool, having fun and finding a girlfriend. Before I even laid my hands on my first commission check – a total of $7,000, which today, let alone 1978, was a nice chunk of cash – I had already mentally spent it on a new stereo, a Caribbean trip and maybe, just maybe, a down payment on a new sports car. So when my manager, a real hard-drinking, hard-living redneck kind of a guy, handed me the check and asked me to go to lunch with him, I thought I was on top of the world. I knew I was paying and I loved it.

# Getting Fired

After downing our burgers and fries, my manager said he had to make a stop before we headed back to the office. He pulled into the garage at 1 Commerce Square, the tallest building in downtown Memphis at that time. As we stepped into the elevator and my manager pushed the button for the top floor, I was still dreaming of buying my dream car, maybe a red Camaro or even a Corvette... When that bell in the elevator rang and the doors opened, though, I saw that we were in the offices of Merrill Lynch. Before I knew it, my boss had commandeered an account rep and steered us towards a desk in the corner. "This young fellow just came into some money," he told the guy from Merrill, who seemed to be taking all of this in stride. "He'd like to open an account." And, before I even knew what was happening, I handed over my check. I can just picture myself: wide-eyed, open-mouthed and speechless. But, you know what, that was one of the best lessons I've ever learned about money. That lesson, to watch your money, which I now recognize with the help of hindsight, also helped me mentally lay the foundation for success in my future small business. It is the key to everything. And, believe it or not, I continue to live off some portion of the proceeds of that first investment even today.

Since all good things must meet their end, AM fizzled away into the nets of its creditors. By 1982, despite my best efforts, the company filed for

# Keep *Swinging*

Chapter 11, signaling that it was high time I rounded up another job. I felt fortunate at the time to land a position with Eastman Kodak in their copy products division, selling high-speed copier systems for $80,000 a pop. It was a heyday in the industry, there was competition everywhere, and I rose to the bait. But I had a lot to overcome at first. Kodak paid its salesman based on a quota of how they improved the book of business from the previous year. Well, the guy I was brought in to replace had done a terrible job with his territory and I had a big hill to climb. Matter of fact, in 1983 I was running negative for the first half of the year because this guy's accounts started dropping us. To make matters worse, Maureen and I had just gotten engaged. I had even bought us a house. Talk about pressure. I was literally driving myself crazy to get things turned around. By doing what I do best, working that shoe leather, I not only ended the year in the black – I had doubled my book of business.

That kind of success got me noticed back in Kodak's headquarters in Rochester, New York. I did so well, in fact, that I was named the company's top salesman in 1984: a real honor. The folks at HQ were so impressed, in fact, that they started talking to me about being on the fast track to a marketing position in Rochester, where Maureen is originally from. The thought of us moving there got her parents very excited and they even started scouting out neighborhoods that would be a good fit for a young couple like us.

# Getting Fired

It took me about six years at Kodak to get to the point of where all the training the company invested in me really began to pay off. I continued to leverage the essential skills I learned over that time period, including simple common sense things like following up with a hand-written note after visiting a prospective client or how to get involved in community activities in order to develop and cultivate leads for new business. I also began to develop the confidence I needed to move past rejection – to develop the resiliency to keep pushing forward. And now I had my eyes set on winning more awards and maybe even securing that executive position back at headquarters in Rochester.

Before I could get there, however, I figured I needed to move out of the copier business, which was rapidly dying out, and move into something more high tech instead. I then positioned myself to get a promotion and a chance to take a leadership role in Kodak's electronic publishing division based in Raleigh, North Carolina. Even though I was now getting ready to be a new dad, I still jumped at the opportunity to take on more responsibility. I even spent five weeks in Rochester in training to prepare for the position when Maureen was in her third trimester. Moving to North Carolina meant I was moving from Memphis to the home of NASCAR and I figured I was on my own fast track. Just 90 days later, however, I wrecked - even though I had just closed a $250,000 deal with a local airline, headquarters made the decision to close my division. I was left stranded in a city where my wife, our baby boy and I knew hardly anyone. When they offered me an entry-level position in Raleigh, after six years of service, I was furious. It was like having a PhD and being sent back to elementary school. My tolerance for working in big company, corporate America was running thin. I recognized that this had become an issue of control: I didn't like someone else pulling my strings. I spent days walking around the house, muttering to myself, "how could they do this to me?" I even had friends in the company calling me up, wondering what had gone wrong. How could one of the company's premier sales guys get such a royal screwing?

By that time, I had earned a reputation for being someone who could get the job done, but maybe would bend a few corporate policies and regulations to get there. I remember a time when a group of colleagues pulled me aside and said, "Jay, you just aren't one to follow the rules. But, in the heat of battle, we sure would like to have you in our foxhole." I really appreciated that and I took it as a compliment: I was a survivor. And I was fed up with Eastman Kodak. I started calling around, but the market for sales and marketing guys in Raleigh and the Research Triangle area in general was thin at that time – the available jobs involved mostly academic work at one of the many universities or technical jobs with the growing number of startups sprouting up in the area. I simply didn't have the experience for any of these jobs.

# Getting Fired

The one upshot of being on Kodak's bench, so to speak, was that I had plenty of free time to make phone calls and hit the links while I was on the company clock: my golf game has never been as good as it was then. While we loved the area, it seemed like it might be tough to land a job with the kind of upside I needed. That's when I decided that we needed to get back to Memphis. To get back home and get reorganized, I took a sales job with Hewlett Packard, but I knew I wasn't long for the job. That was the one and only time that I took a job for purely selfish reasons: I wanted them to move me and Maureen back home and I wanted a high-tech job on my resume.

I took advantage of what HP would give me. I challenged myself to take every training class I could on mini-computers. I even traveled all over the country, from Cupertino, California to Atlanta working my shoe leather. I traveled so much during that time, in fact, that when Maureen found out she was pregnant with our daughter Katie, she and her sister Molly joked that it wasn't possible because I hadn't been home in months. I wasn't laughing.

After about two years on the job, I started daydreaming again about trying something new. I had come across this relatively new outfit in town called ATS; a telecom company that was in the market for some computers. After doing some research on them, I liked what I saw, especially compared to what I was looking at by staying on at HP. While the company was obviously doing well, it was filled with engineers and not a lot of marketing folks. I just didn't fit in. But when I talked to some friends and clients, they thought I was nuts: why would you ever leave a safe secure Fortune 500 firm like HP, especially for a relative startup? I knew it was a big risk.

In 1990, just about two years after we moved back to Memphis, I made the decision to leave HP and challenged myself again by taking a job with ATS as a data products manager. The position was touted as "The Opportunity of a Lifetime." I was to head up their voice recognition products division – the kinds of artificial intelligence systems that read you back your account balance when you call up your bank in the middle of the night. While the technology was interesting, I quickly realized that ATS just didn't have enough programmers to make a serious go of it. Fortunately, a few weeks later my boss, Bob Chance, dropped a video on my desk and asked me to check it out. The video was some promotional material from a company called Video Telecom, which was one of the early leaders in building something called video conferencing systems. I fell in love immediately: I just thought it was so cool to see two people in completely different cities talking to each other. Even better, the company was backed by a group of local investors who had a track record for backing winners. I even brought the tape home to show Maureen. Not only was this technology cool, I could see how it could help companies cut down on unnecessary travel or to help teach kids who lived in remote areas. The more and more I studied the potential of these systems, the more excited I got. It became my passion.

# Getting Fired

While I had learned to sell technology over the past 12 years, I still didn't know all that much about how it worked. Now, my job was not just to be a salesman, but I was going to have to be the installer, trainer and tech support guy all rolled into one. I'll admit I was nervous, but I also saw an opportunity to build a business of my own within a business around some technology that nobody knew much of anything about. I worked my tail off, staying late every night and trudging into the office on weekends to read manuals, take the demo equipment apart and to call up the manufacturer's tech support teams to learn everything I could about how this equipment functioned. I was like a tornado – sucking up every bit of information I could. While ATS was paying me a decent salary, I was earning ten-times that in the education I was receiving not only in the technology, but also in learning how to run my own business unit, how to manage cash flow and making contacts throughout the industry. While I didn't realize it at the time, I was building the foundation for the skills I needed to run my own business someday.

And all that hard work paid off for ATS as well. Within the first year, I landed the distance learning centers at the University of Tennessee and the University of Memphis as clients. Over the next five years, in fact, I landed just about every college and university in the states of Alabama, Mississippi and Tennessee as well, which helped my division grow to about $5 million a year in sales. I began to really see the future of where this technology could go – education, health care, corporate communi-

# Keep *Swinging*

cations – and I thought the CEO of the company was behind me 100 percent. Boy, was I wrong.

*December 8, 1995*

Here I was excited that my boss asked me out to lunch on my birthday. My division at ATS was growing like gangbusters and I had a few ideas I wanted to run by him about how to grow it even faster. The potential for this technology is limitless, I told him. But he just sat there, quiet, avoiding my eyes. Before we could even order any food, he let me have it. "Jay, we're going to have to let you go," he mumbled. I couldn't believe what I was hearing. "You're letting me go? Are you kidding me, after everything I have done for you?" I was stunned. It was truly as if he had kicked me in the gut. I was humiliated. While I admit that we hadn't been getting along well over the past few months, I never thought he would stoop this low, to give up just when we were starting to get ahead. It turns out things were getting bad at ATS financially and they were cutting back wherever they could. My division was making money, we were profitable - I thought we could turn things around. He had other ideas.

Getting fired, on my birthday, just a few weeks before the holidays no less, left me cold. I felt like I was caught in a downward spiral that lasted for weeks. They had given me six weeks worth of severance pay and by about

# Getting Fired

Valentine's Day, it was just about gone. I started working my network, called up the video conference equipment manufacturers to see if I could land a job with them. Nobody seemed interested, however, and my depression darkened. I started wondering what God had in mind for me.

While I had played with the idea of opening my own business, I didn't have the money to start it up and I knew I couldn't go to my brother or father for help either; as employees of the Better Business Bureau, they were public servants and they just didn't have the kind of money I needed to make a sizable investment in this kind of high-tech equipment. With my severance running thin, I was also in hurry-up mode: I didn't have time to go through the traditional routes most people take like applying for a Small Business Administration loan or something. I did talk to a few banks, but because they didn't understand the technology, they weren't going to take a risk on me.

That's when I caught a break. A friend of mine I met through Junior Achievement, a volunteer-run organization that teaches young people about running a business, introduced me to a local Memphis financier who was looking for investment opportunities. This investor liked my story and said he would take a look at my business plan. Business plan? I didn't have a business plan and I really didn't even know how to begin one. To make matters worse, I didn't even have a typewriter, let alone a computer. Some high tech whiz, huh? So I called up my brother John, who was president of the Memphis Better Business Bureau, and asked him if I could use his word processor. Of course, he told me, so I hopped in my car and headed to his office.

Let me jump ahead a bit to March 1996, spare you some of the drama involved in making a pitch to investors, and let you know that I raised about $70,000 in seed money from that investor and some of his partners. I still don't know if they did it for pity, curiosity or whether they really thought I was on to something. What I can admit now is that they made that investment based on the most ragged business plan of all time. How ragged? I actually typed up my pro-forma numbers on some paper I took from my Franklin Planner. Nevertheless, I had my startup capital. I rented a small office, just a couple hundred square feet, which was soon filled up with some demo equipment. I even reached out to one of my buddies back at ATS, an engineer who was a real genius with video technology since I knew I was going to need some help. He said he was interested, but he needed a few months before he could join me full time. In other words, he wanted to see that I had some sales lined up first. I couldn't blame him. So I hit the phones: I used the Memphis Business Journal listings to canvas all the companies I thought could be interested in my technology. I knew I had a nice little niche and it was relatively easy to get people's attention. I was also scared – and excited – as hell. Fate had forced me into this position: if I couldn't land another corporate job, I had to create my own to provide for me and my fam-

# Getting Fired

ily. This was the spark I needed to get off the ground; maybe I wouldn't have taken the risk otherwise. It had taken me 18 years to reach this point on my entrepreneurial journey and it was time to finally establish some control over my life. I remember telling Maureen that I had come to a fork in the road and I already knew that one path hadn't worked, so it was time to try the other one. And that's how Interactive Solutions got its start.

*Pro Forma – Videoconferencing Company* (financial spreadsheet, largely illegible)

*ISI's First Business Plan (Pro Forma) Typewritten on a Franklin Planner but it did get us started*

# Chapter Three

# STARTUP PROBLEMS

*The fight for survival*

I have to admit that in the earliest days of ISI, part of the fuel that kept me going was anger: anger at the way I had been dumped by ATS. But I was too busy to dwell on my feelings for very long. Everything was happening so fast: the hurry-up business plan, landing the investors, renting an office. I was also somewhat blind to the challenges before me; I thought I had the experience to ride out a few speed bumps. I had no idea what we were in store for.

It was about that time that my brother John pulled me aside and gave me some sage advice: "You're in for the fight of your life little brother." John had a failed business on his resume, and I knew he was speaking from experience. He and two partners had started an art supply and framing business after he graduated from college, even though he knew just about nothing about either the art business or about framing. The company and the partnership flamed out after about three years, leaving my brother severely in debt, enough so that he was forced to declare bankruptcy at the age of 23. Needless to say, it was a long time before he could afford a house of his own. He told me, in short, to check my ego at the door and do whatever I needed to do to make ISI a success. And in the beginning, I was a solo act, constantly working the phones to drum up some clients so that I could line up some work so my friend the engineer could leave ATS and join me at ISI. Since he was working from his home in Kentucky, our only contact was by phone anyway. But, by May, 1996, I had given him a stake in the company – 17.5 percent, same as my own, and I was anxious to start earning a return to our investors who owned the rest.

My biggest hurdle in the beginning was educating the general public about what this video conferencing technology was all about exactly. And, since I had signed a non-compete with ATS saying I wouldn't call on my old customers in the colleges and universities, I needed to strike out in a new direction. That's when it hit me: we could go after commercial clients instead of these academic institutions. Rather than limit ourselves to distance learning, we could become a video conferencing and audio-visual engineering company that offered sales support along with the insight into new and emerging technologies. We would offer our clients the research capabilities and expertise into exciting new technologies and applications that they simply couldn't afford to have in house. That meant that we were a reseller, but we would be vendor agnostic – we wouldn't get tied in too heavily to any one product set so that we could offer our customer objective opinions on the best technol-

# Startup Problems

ogy at the best price. We actually struggled to nail down a name and logo for the company at first: we tossed out quite a few names like Video Visions and Video Innovations before deciding on Interactive Solutions, partly because it didn't tie us down to selling only video products. We wanted to be a provider of technology and engineering solutions that had a particular expertise in video conferencing. That's also why our original logo used big, chunky letters so that people would think of us like an engineering firm.

The problem was that I didn't have the money or the sales force to spread the word as quickly as I needed. And, when I did find someone willing to listen to my pitch, I wanted to sound bigger and more established than we were. It's like the old military strategy of making two look like 200. I needed to find some creative ways to partner up with someone who could help ISI seem both legitimate and larger than it really was. As the old adage says, necessity is the mother of invention and sometimes you never know how you'll take advantage.

In my time in that office, I also came up with the idea of reaching out to our neighbors in the office park we worked in, one of which happened to be MCI, which was still a big deal in the telecom world at that time. As I got to know some of the sales reps over there, I realized that they were a great source of potential customers of ISI: they served the kinds of businesses that might be interested in what I was selling. I had tried to sell the concept of video technology to MCI directly, but at that time at least, they only wanted to sell their network. It was the same story at the other big communication companies like Sprint and AT&T, they were too distracted – they didn't have the time and desire to get into this stuff in a big way. The sales reps, on the other hand, saw things differently. We actually landed our first serious sales call, Buckeye Technologies in Memphis, on a lead we got through an MCI sales rep. She had been nice enough to mention ISI to her contact over there and we took over. I did what I thought was right and gave that a rep a piece of the action. And as word spread, we started landing all kinds of leads out of MCI.

Even though we were making headway, it still wasn't enough for our investors. My partner and I would do weekly conference calls with them to fill them in on our progress, like the fact that we had a hot lead with Buckeye, but after a while we could tell something was wrong. We could almost feel the chill through the phone. Then, in June, just three months after they agreed to back us, our investors decided they had seen enough: they wanted their money back, which amounted to about $70,000. They had pulled the rug out from under us, leaving me, yet again, to scramble to keep things together.

# Startup Problems

This is where I have to give my partner a lot of credit. I knew we didn't have a chance of getting a bank or SBA loan, we had been down that road already, but my partner set up a meeting with his father. After hearing our pitch, my partner's father, who had done well for himself, agreed to co-sign a loan for $125,000 from the People's Bank in Murray, Kentucky. While that amount allowed us to pay off our investors, we were left with just $55,000 to get the company off the ground. It didn't look good. We did owe those investors a debt of gratitude though: those investors didn't ask for any interest on their $70,000. So, while we had to scramble to make good on it, it had basically added up to a free three-month loan and in those three months we were able to prove that there was something to this business. And now – we were 50/50 partners. If we could pull this off, we stood to gain significantly more as owners. Now, we just had to find some people willing to pay for our products and services.

And it was actually my brother John who pointed out to me that losing our investors was the best thing that could have happened to us. After he said that, though, I was like, huh? "John buddy, I love you, but could you please explain how scrambling to get a loan to pay off those guys was a good thing?" I said. "Think about it," he explained patiently. "They basically just gave you a 90-day, interest free loan to prove the concept of your business. You couldn't have gotten that loan without having the customer prospects you have now. Plus, you just tripled your ownership

# Keep *Swinging*

stake in the company and it didn't cost you a penny." As usual, John saw something that I had missed. He was right: I shouldn't harbor any ill will towards those investors; I should be praising them for giving us credibility instead. We were carving out a spot in a fledgling industry and they had given us our start. I slapped my brother on the back, got a smile back on my face and started thinking about how we were going to land some customers; we needed to start paying back that loan.

Then, about a month later, Maureen and I took a long weekend and went up to my partner's family lake house in Kentucky to relax a bit. I remember lounging around and watching the 1996 Summer Olympics on TV. That's when the unthinkable happened: the phone rang and it was the folks from Buckeye on the other end of the line. They wanted to do a deal with us with a price tag of $155,000. Jackpot! I just about hit my knees in thanks: the timing couldn't have been any better. The strange thing about that day was that as Maureen and I were celebrating, my partner and his wife seemed very nonchalant about the whole deal. Their attitude was like, oh yeah, we expected this to happen. I'm thinking: Are these people serious? We just landed our first big deal, one we had to have to make the bank happy, and that's how you react? Looking back on that day today, I recognize that the first seeds were sown in what would soon erupt into a real problem between my partner and me. But more on that later.

# Startup Problems

First things first: we had our first client. But, as I mentioned earlier, we had very little capital to work with, especially to front the costs for the kind of equipment Buckeye was looking at. In other words, we didn't have enough money or credit to buy the equipment from the vendors. We would have been in trouble if I hadn't somehow negotiated an 80 percent down payment from Buckeye, which is basically unheard of, especially for a startup like we were. Buckeye wasn't happy paying it, but we justified it telling them that we needed it to cover the up-front labor and equipment costs. We also let them hold onto the remaining 20 percent until the project was completed. This was really my first lesson in how important cash is to a business: as the old saying goes, cash is king. Getting as much of a contract up front not only allowed us to stay afloat, it gave us more leeway to borrow from banks (they love to see cash flow) and it was a lesson we used over and over again to stay afloat and fight another day.

Little did I know that my survival skills were going to be put to the test yet again, albeit in an unexpected way. Not long after we landed Buckeye as a client, I went to get my hair cut. It was there that Elaine, my barber, asked if I had bumped my head. "No," I said. "Why?" "Well you have a dark patch of skin on your scalp that looks like a bruise," she said. I didn't think much of it, but I asked Maureen to take a look at it anyway after I got home. After taking a look, she said, let's go see the dermatologist. After a few weeks of painful testing – the docs sliced me up pretty good to get their samples – the verdict was in: cancer. Melanoma to be specific, a particularly deadly variety of cancer that kills about 10 percent of people that get it. Though I'm fair-skinned and have lived in the hot climate of the south, I was still shocked. I thought I was pretty good about wearing hats and sunscreen whenever I was outside for any amount of time. The docs told me that this was the kind of thing that might have been building for years – could have been from too many sunburns from when I was younger. That's also when they started using another word I don't like much: surgery. I have to admit, I was scared. Scared that I might abandon my wife and two children. Scared that all I had done to get ISI off the ground was now in vain. Scared, quite frankly, to die.

But, I knew my best chance to live was to go through with the surgery. With Maureen and the kids' support, I mustered up the courage and reported for surgery. And, after the cutting and the stitching, the skin grafts and the staples were finished, I was left with a silver-dollar-sized dent in my head. "We think we got it all," the docs told me. While I know they meant well, a cancer diagnosis plays mind games with you. It was hard to shake the feelings of doom, that I wouldn't see all my dreams come true. It was a tough situation. Rather than dwell on it too much, I plowed my worries into my work instead. The next Tuesday, just three days after the surgery, I conducted a demo in my office with a ball-cap on and with the help of a fistful of painkillers. I didn't want to bury my

# Startup Problems

head in the sand and I felt like it was good therapy to keep working since it kept me from thinking about the cancer.

I was also proving something to myself, proving that I could keep working towards making ISI a success. By the end of the year, we had a lot of people buzzing around our products, but we hadn't been able to close a lot of business. While we had landed another client, Computer Services Inc. in Paducah, Kentucky, that helped pushed our annual revenues to $260,000; we still ended up losing $82,000 for the year, partly because my partner had forked over more than $13,000 to a bogus supplier up in New Hampshire. My partner had ordered some parts from them for the work we were doing on a crazy new project in Memphis. Not only did they not deliver the parts, they skipped town. I was ashamed: Here I was from a family with two members in the Better Business Bureau and we never even checked these guys out. I had harsh words for my partner that day to be sure.

As the holidays rolled around, and our first year in business began to wrap up, it was time to take stock of what I had accomplished, if anything. For one, I felt beat up - just completely exhausted, both mentally and physically. I went to visit my dad in his office to chat. As we sat around his office drinking Cokes, I related everything that had happened over the past year: getting fired, landing the investors, starting the business, losing the investors, the cancer and, to top things off, my partner blew a good chunk of our cash on a bogus supplier. "God must really be pissed at me," I said. He kind of chuckled and put his arm on my shoulder. "I hear you," he said. "You have been through a lot. He's testing you and you have to decide what to do about it. Maybe it is time to fold up your tent. Or just maybe it's time for you to step it up." He gave my shoulder a good squeeze and then got back to his Coke. He was right of course. My dad was a man who used simple words, but gave great advice. I remember too when, after I had just started the company, I still hadn't gotten over getting fired by ATS. I mean it had never happened before and my pride was at stake. After spouting off for a while about my boss, he did the same thing: put his hand on my shoulder and gave me a squeeze. "Those folks definitely did you wrong," he told me. "But here's the thing: to make yourself successful, you need more than just anger. People don't like dealing with angry people. They like upbeat motivated people that they can trust and get enthusiastic about."

My dad was right again, of course. He reminded me about an old adage he had heard once that went something like, he who seeks revenge digs two graves. Starting ISI wasn't about getting back at anyone at ATS; it was about creating a successful business and gaining my independence from the corporate world.

# Startup Problems

So, when I take the time now to reflect on my first year as an entrepreneur, and with the benefit of some hindsight, what did I learn? First off, things would have been a heck of a lot easier if I knew more people willing to lend me some money. Ideally, I would've married into it - just kidding, Maureen, (kind of). If I had more time, I would definitely have explored an SBA loan or reached out to angel investors, wealthy individuals and former entrepreneurs willing to stake a new venture, who are much more approachable today. I would also have thought out my partnership split better than to end up with only 17 percent. I wish I had taken more time to develop a high-quality, well-thought-out business plan. If you approach any investor without one, you're dead on arrival. That business plan can also serve as a long-term road map to help you steer through some of the bumps we quickly ran into in terms of our strategy, location and money – the lack thereof. Cash is king in a startup and I learned early on that you skimp on things as long as you have to, even if that means buying used equipment, get the cheapest insurance and always, always get as much money up front from a customer as you can. If we hadn't negotiated that deal with Buckeye to pay us 80 percent up front, ISI might not have made it. And that's part of the notion that you have to fake it till you make it in the beginning. We always tried to seem bigger than we were and because we skimped on hiring any sales people besides me, rounding up those MCI folks to vouch for us made a huge deal.

# Keep *Swinging*

So, looking back, I learned a lot that first year, especially about myself. I now knew I had the intestinal fortitude to withstand just about anything that came my way. Maybe I gained some courage by thinking, mistakenly, that it all was downhill from that point. And maybe God was indeed testing me. But the worst day I ever had working at ISI would still rank among the best of those that I worked as a corporate drone: this was all mine and nobody was telling me what to do. To really get there though, to have the sense of ownership that I craved, I first had to have a reckoning with my partner, the engineer.

*One of ISI's First Clients – It was only a $28,000 order, but in June of 1996 it felt like $28 million.*

# Chapter Four

# BREAKING AWAY

## *Surviving Professional Divorce*

*March 1997*

I hang up the phone and sigh. Another phone call with my business partner results in yet another disagreement. In hindsight, I think, things would have been so much better if I had never brought him into the business. The stakes are getting bigger and his mistakes are starting to cost us. We started the business together but it seems like we want different things out of it today. I'm beginning to dread each and every time we have to talk. I'm sitting here in Memphis, a city of a million people, where our employees are, where potential million-dollar customers like FedEx and AutoZone are. He's out there in Murray, Kentucky – way out in the country – because he's a small town guy who wants to be close to his family. While I respect that, it is not what's best for the business. We need to be here in Memphis to grow, to recruit both employees and land new customers. Why can't he understand that? I sigh again. We just aren't on the same page anymore. I wonder - Would I be any better on my own?

When I recruited my friend from ATS back in 1996, it just made sense. I am first and foremost a sales and marketing guy. My role is to bring the energy, the sizzle. I wanted to start a technology business, so I knew I needed to team up with a strong, experienced techie guru to make sure we were operating on the cutting edge and who could install the sophisticated equipment I was selling. I needed someone who could provide the steak. This was the second time I had hired my friend: I tapped him to be my first video systems engineer for ATS. He was a crackerjack when it came to these video conferencing and networking gadgets I had such high hopes for.

Like me, my partner was always a family guy. He was a Kentucky man through and through. After getting his degree at Murray State, which was housed in the town he insisted on staying in, he stayed on for seven years, helping expand the university's network around the state. He further developed his expertise working on networking projects for the U.S. Navy and the states of Alabama, Virginia and Georgia. In other words, he was a real pro at video networking as well as the associated hardware and software. I also thought he was a good guy, someone I thought I could trust to start a new business with. I started talking to him about my idea for a company, thinking he would be the perfect partner to start it with. And, looking back, if it hadn't been for his dad co-signing that loan with the People's Bank in Murray, ISI might not exist at all.

The tradeoff, of course, was that my partner worked from a second office we set up in Murray. That meant that, right off the bat, we had doubled

# Breaking Away

the overhead and the challenge of coordinating communications between our technical base in Murray and our sales headquarters of sorts in Memphis. At the time, we felt that having two offices would enable us to go after customers in two states. The idea was that I would sell out of my office and my partner would assemble the products in his, then travel to Memphis when it was time to do the install. Whenever he was in Memphis, or I was in Murray, it was assumed we would stay at each other's house. It didn't take long before our long-distance relationship led to some trouble.

In the early days, I spent my time selling video conferencing systems to whomever I thought would need them and be able to pay for them. In short, I was selling the promise of technology that made long-distance video communications routine and affordable. My partner was in charge of initial hardware testing, systems installation as well as keeping himself educated and up to date on the capabilities of the latest and greatest technology. He was also responsible for overseeing our spare parts and equipment inventory as well as systems design.

Towards the end of 1996, he came away impressed by the potential of some new video transmission components that we needed to complete a critical system installation which was made by a business in New Hampshire. He had to have it, he told me, and subsequently asked me to put a check in the mail for $13,368 for an advance order on a few units. Now, at this point, we were at the tail end of our start up year, had been through a lot of ups and downs and had perhaps $50,000 in the bank that represented the balance of funds after refinancing the company back in July. My partner knew all of this, but nonetheless insisted that the $13,000 was an investment in our company's future with an exciting new application.

The rub was that the business in New Hampshire flamed out before they ever delivered a single circuit board to us. The company was, in fact, bogus and had bilked a number of companies like ours out of hundreds of thousands of dollars over the past few years. Shortly after we sent our money to them, I had even received a call from the New Hampshire Attorney General's office questioning why we did business with this firm. I felt foolish - I was also furious. "How could you risk that much of our capital on something so risky", I asked my partner after learning the devastating news. He, of course, had no good answer. "It was the best technology available," he fired back. "Our customer needed it for their system," he said. "A lot of good it's doing them." Then he said something that really blew me away: "Heck, just "write the $13,000 off." I was speechless. Rather than respond to such a naïve statement, I slammed the phone down instead. I know that if I had been sitting next to him, I would never have allowed him to write that check. Little did I know that this realization would be a turning point: the beginning of the end of our partnership.

# Breaking Away

A few months later, towards the end of our second year in business, we were picking up momentum. Sales had quadrupled over the first year, cracking the magical $1 million-dollar mark that, to us, made it seem that we might actually be onto something real. It even looked like, if things broke right, we might be able to pocket a bit of profit. That was the good news. The bad news was that my partner and I continued to struggle running the business efficiently from two locations. As a numbers guy, I couldn't stop thinking about what our profits could have been if we weren't springing for duplicate costs like multiple rents, extra travel, and two telephones. Because we bought things like computers and office supplies from different vendors, we couldn't even negotiate with them for discounts. There had to be a better way to run a business, I thought to myself.

The problem was that my partner refused to move his family. I approached him on several occasions, pitching him on my ideas about the efficiencies we could gain from working in the same office and the potential new business we could track down in the Memphis area. He was happy where he was, he said, and the company was doing fine. Faced with his resolve, there wasn't much I could do, I thought. I need him for his technical skills and he needs me for my sales and marketing savvy. So, rather than battling further, I picked up my own efforts to grow the company.

# Keep *Swinging*

A few days later, after we both attended a big Christmas party celebration at a local restaurant, my partner and I had to make a long Sunday drive to Atlanta to deal with yet another customer complaint. It was a complicated issue regarding some hardware that had been ordered. To make matters even worse, we were traveling on a Sunday because we were scheduled to meet our customers in his office at 5:30 a.m. on a Monday morning to discuss the problem. Not only was I upset that my partner had dragged us into yet another problem, I was dreading getting up that early to solve it. I was on a slow burn the whole time we were in Atlanta - and on the entire return drive back home to Memphis. Driving time is my thinking time and I couldn't get past the fact that my partner and I continued to take money out of our own pockets by maintaining two offices. To make matters worse, my partner continued to botch critical details like forgetting expensive parts for systems (like that client in Atlanta), taking too long to test systems in Murray, wasting what money we had on a variety of things like new computers and software. It wasn't a good feeling. We were a small business in 1997 but we were getting bigger and I noticed for the first time that we started to receive complaints from customers and vendors. The gripes – which began to threaten our reputation - included things like slow delivery times and mistakes in configurations of customer systems. I counted up the damage his mistakes had cost us: I stopped when I got to about $40,000. This was coming from the guy who had just recently told me that he couldn't wait to retire based on the success of the company.

# Breaking Away

Retire? What in the heck are you thinking? I thought at the time. Here he is costing the company money and he is already looking to get out of the business. That's when it hit me clear as day: I needed to do this on my own. Yes - I needed to buy my partner out, I said out loud. It was the first time in a while that I smiled when I thought of him.

Even though I was relieved at my revelation, I soon came to realize that ending a partnership is easier said than done. As many people have since told me, ending a partnership can be even harder than ending a marriage.

Soon after that decisive drive back from Atlanta, I mailed my partner a letter to feel him out about restructuring the company's ownership. In other words, I offered to buy him out. Imagine my surprise when, two days later, my partner and his wife show up on my doorstep demanding to know what was going on. He was absolutely furious. He began shouting, asking who in the hell I thought I was, and saying that I didn't have a company without him. You couldn't afford to buy me out, he barked. I'll admit it threw me off a bit and things quickly deteriorated from there. It was very difficult for both of us to keep our emotions under control. We were friendly after all. But in partnerships, finding that fine line between personal and professional is awfully difficult to come by and it gets ugly quick.

# Keep *Swinging*

Our problem was made worse because, as I'm told is the case in many partnerships, we failed to agree to a buy-sell agreement when we founded the company. Such a contract should spell out in clear black and white how the company can be dissolved should one or both of the partners decide to sell their interests in the business. The problem, of course, is that when you're in the thrilling stages of launching a new company, the last thing you want to talk about with your partner is legal language that describes how you can dissolve the business equitably. While Maureen and I never dealt with a pre-nuptial agreement, I hear they're not popular for the exact same reasons. So, when it came to me and my partner settling over our business divorce, we had only one option to turn to in resolving our differences: Lawyers, lots and lots of expensive lawyers.

After that impromptu and emotional conversation at my house, which happened in early 1998, my partner and I began conducting most of our correspondence through our lawyers. After hearing me out, my partner had said, "you don't want me in the company, fine, but you're going to have to make me happy." I knew what that meant: money. I, on the other hand, wanted to pay him as little as possible. We had only recently begun to pay ourselves any kind of salary and money was tight all around. He, of course, still had his dreams of becoming a millionaire. We were stuck.

# Breaking Away

We actually did try another means of solving our dispute and that was to use a mediator. Mediators, often "off-duty" lawyers, are basically consultants that help broker disputes between two parties like my partner and me. Mediators not only charge less per hour than lawyers on retainer, their goal is to help you avoid heading to the courtroom to resolve the dispute. Our mediator experience, however, was a disaster. My brother, John recommended someone that had done some work for the Better Business Bureau - a well-regarded female mediator based out of Memphis. About a week later, after we batted some preliminary numbers back and forth, I get a call from my partner. "You're trying to take advantage of me," he yelled into the phone, "That woman went to high school with you." Again, I was taken aback by my partner's emotions, which were evolving into paranoia. The mediator had indeed gone to a school, Christian Brothers University, with a similar name as my alma mater, Christian Brothers High School. My partner, however, failed to recognize that my high school had an all-male enrollment. I decided not to try and explain this subtle fact to him and hung up. So ended our experience with mediation. Needless to say, it was a lousy one.

About three months later, we did reach a settlement but not before yet another confrontation between my partner and me. He threatened me, threatened to liquidate me for trying to take the company away from him. I truly regret that our partnership came down to that moment, came down to him feeling like I was intentionally trying to ruin him in some way. In hindsight, there are so many things we could have done differently to avoid the emotion and the mistrust. In the end, my partner settled for much less than his million dollars, I can't divulge specific figures as to the payout to my partner, but I did have to come up with over $250,000 in order to refinance the company's debt and deal with expenses related to the partnership split.

The problem was that I didn't have anything close to $250,000 on hand at the time. I literally turned over every stone I could to raise the money: I took out a second mortgage and a home equity line of $75,000 on our home; I took out a loan with 12 percent interest for $35,000; I borrowed the entire balance - $65,000 - from my 401(k) account. I even had to turn to my brother-in-law in Nashville to help co-sign on a note for $75,000.

At the same time, I now found myself in a precarious position. I was flying solo for the first time in my professional career. It was exhilarating. I was also scared to death: I now had $250,000 in debt to make good on in addition to running the company. Not only did I have a bank loan to make good on, I had also leveraged everything I could get my hands on from the house, to our cars to my retirement plan to make this plan work. I was all that stood between the company's survival - and my family's future financial well being as well. If the company and I failed to deliver, I was looking at bankruptcy.

# Breaking Away

I couldn't help but wonder if I had made the best decision for the company and my family. Was I as capable of doing all of this as I thought just a few months ago? What about my customers, my suppliers - are they going to wonder the same thing? Can we really rely on this guy to do business with, they would say? I imagined them thinking that my partner, the engineer was the real brains behind the company. I had awful, sweaty nightmares about all of my customers leaving me at once. Even when I woke up, cold and clammy, it still felt like it was happening, like it was real. Doubt can be a nasty enemy.

At the same time, I felt relieved and liberated. I had something to prove, not only to my father, my brother, and myself, but also to my previous employers and co-workers. I was going to show them what I was all about. And I trusted myself to make good decisions, foremost among them hiring Derek Plummer, ISI's new chief engineer, and Don Cottam, the company's new sales guy, right in the middle of the buyout. Neither guy had a lick of experience in the industry, but I had a great feeling about each of them. (More on them later.) More importantly, truly for the first time in my career, I felt like I was building a team and I loved it.

# Keep *Swinging*

*Suddenly Solo- The new ISI team and the Collierville Chamber of Commerce cele-brating our new office on Hwy 72.*

*ISI Goes Global- A video conferencing installation in Dublin, Ireland-Moments like this after the partnership split made me feel like we were going somewhere.*

# Chapter Five

# SECRET WEAPONS

*Who to turn to when you need advice*

I'm sitting down at my desk when just an ordinary day became something a whole lot more. I'll admit I was a bit excited about the great write-up we had just received in the Memphis Business Journal and I was looking forward to seeing what kind of business that free PR might drum up. I couldn't help but break out into a big grin. I snapped out of my daydream when my phone rings and my receptionist tells me that there is a Mr. Kemmons Wilson on the phone for me. "Yeah, right," I say as I pick up the phone anyway, figuring it's a buddy of mine calling up to rib me a bit about the article. "Hello Mr. Myers," the voice at the other end of the line says. "This is Kemmons Wilson. Not sure if you know who I am, but I just read about your company back there in Memphis and it sounds like you've got some neat stuff I'd like to talk to you about." I was stunned. Kemmons Wilson, the founder of Holiday Inns. A local legend. Calling me. To ask for an appointment? Wow. "Hello?" "Sorry Mr. Wilson. Uh, would you like to stop by later this week?" I asked. "Well actually, I'm up in my jet at the moment, somewhere over North Dakota I

57

think, and I thought I'd drop by this afternoon. Does that work for you?" "Yes sir, sure, we'll be here," I stuttered in response. I don't know how long I sat there with that phone stuck to my ear, listening to nothing but a dial tone on the other end. Kemmons Wilson, coming here, to meet me. Wow. I told my secretary to go out and buy a camera so we could take some pictures. "This is a rare moment in time," I told her. The budding entrepreneur meets the legend.

You might not expect that Memphis has been the launching pad for a long series of entrepreneurial success stories. Sure, most folks know about Fred Smith, the man who started by operating 14 small delivery aircraft out of the Memphis International Airport in 1973, and who now heads up a company with more than $34 billion in annual revenues called FedEx. When you take an even closer look at the distinguished list of inductees in a local Memphis organization called the Society of Entrepreneurs, though, you might be surprised to learn that Memphis resident Abe Plough turned a $125 loan from his father into what is today, the Schering-Plough Corporation, the pharmaceutical and consumer product manufacturer that sold some $10.4 billion worth of St. Joseph's aspirin, Dr. Scholl's foot powder and Maybelline cosmetics last year. And where would grocery stores be today if not for Clarence Saunders and Piggly Wiggly? Piggly Wiggly is the grocery store chain he founded in downtown Memphis in 1916 that brought us

# Secret Weapons

innovations like self-service shopping and refrigerated produce cases. Memphis tourists can also thank Mr. Saunders for the Pink Palace museum, named for its walls made of pink Georgia marble, which at one time, Mr. Saunders had intended to be his dream home. And the list goes on: How about J.R. (Pitt) Hyde III, the founder of AutoZone, or cotton king William Dunavant? Sure, this is no who's who of Silicon Valley, but they are the men who turned everyday industries into extraordinary ones. My favorite standout on that list has always been Kemmons Wilson, the man who, after growing frustrated with the lack of affordable and reliable lodging on a family trip from Memphis to Washington in 1951, built the first of what are today more than 1,400 Holiday Inns worldwide.

The thing that always drew me to Mr. Wilson's story was that it lacked the glitz of so many of today's big success stories. This was a man who earned every penny he ever made the hard way. Mr. Wilson, whose full name is actually Charles Kemmons Wilson, was born in Osceola, Arkansas, but his mother and he moved to Memphis in 1913 when he was only 9 months old, after his father passed away. While school didn't seem to suit him (no Harvard MBA here), Mr. Wilson quit going when he was 14, he was always working odd jobs like as a delivery boy, operating a popcorn machine at a movie theatre and later a pinball-machine business to support his mother. One of the favorite tips he was known for saying was, "Work only half a day; it makes no difference which half – it can be either the first 12 hours or the last 12 hours." This was a man who knew how to hustle. And, after opening that first hotel on Summer Avenue in Memphis, which he named after Bing Crosby's famous movie Holiday Inn, he used that hustle to change the way Americans traveled in their country: By 1964, there were more than 500 Holiday Inns around the country and, about 20 years after that, he opened 1,100 more – making Holiday Inns the largest hotel and motel operation in the world at the time. Mr. Wilson, who was known as much for his generosity as he was for his trademark wide grin, donated some $15 million to my alma mater, The University of Memphis, to build the Kemmons Wilson School of Hospitality and Resort Management, a working hotel on campus that I knew well: this man was a legend in every sense of the word.

So imagine my utter surprise when the still-spry 83-year-old Mr. Wilson showed up in my office that day. I was so pumped up about his visit that, when he first came in, I wasn't sure whether to bow or shake his hand. Interestingly enough while we did talk a bit about his interest in outfitting a few hotels with my video conferencing systems, he was actually more interested in just having a good chat. He shared a few stories of his struggles from the early days and patiently listened to a few of my own. All in all, he stayed for about an hour, but before he left, he said, "You hang in here. You're going to make some money in this business." Man was that an inspirational moment. I ended up talking to Mr.

# Secret Weapons

Wilson several more times over the next year or so before he passed away at the age of 90 in 2003. He always made it seem like he just might want to buy some equipment, but he never did. I suspect he would stop in on other businesses like mine just to chat and share some advice from his experiences. He worked until he died and he never lost his enthusiasm for life and the business world. And I'll never forget a few gems of advice he gave me: hire good people and then let them do their job. If you hire the right people, he told me, you won't have to look over their shoulder and do their work for them. Also, he said, don't fall into the trap of hiring people that are just like you and have the same skill-sets. You need a variety of talent to make a business successful. I continue to heed that advice and it has resulted in assembling as fine a team of talent as there is in the business. And the price of that advice: nothing, except a few minutes of my time.

Looking back at both my career and my life in general, I can't overstate the importance that other people – friends, family, and mentors like Mr. Wilson – have played in helping me steer ISI through the good times and the bad: those consultants, both paid and unpaid, willing to lend me their ear and some quality advice in shaping ISI's future. If I have a single strength as an entrepreneur, I will say that I have never been too proud to accept the wisdom from people that have already been there, done that – and I have often been willing to pay for that wisdom. Some people, in fact, can be quite flattered when asked for help – and they don't send you a six-figure bill in return. When I have accepted awards on behalf of the company in the past, for instance, I have often felt like an Oscar winner, rattling on and on about all the people I wanted to thank. And my father and brother John have always stood at the top of that list. While my family didn't have the money to lend me to finance my business, I am unable to put a value on the advice and counsel they provided me over the first turbulent years of ISI.

I continue to feel the loss of both my father and my brother with just about every day that goes by. My dad passed away in 1999, my brother, more tragically, and unexpectedly, at the age of 50 in 2002. They had each served as the president of the Better Business Bureau in Memphis, and the best way to describe their influence on me is that they were basically my Bibles. My dad was the Old Testament; my brother was the New Testament. In other words, my dad was very traditional in the wear-a-suit-and-tie-everyday kind of way while my brother was more modern, more relaxed, and embraced technology in every way he could. Their differences only served to balance each other and they in turn helped bring balance to me. They both advised me, of course, to make sure that my business had a good name and reputation with the BBB and that it was ok to take on some risk: the safe route was the one that everyone else took. They told me that even if your business is small, look big-

# Secret Weapons

ger by dressing professionally. "But I'm in the tech business, that doesn't mean as much anymore," I protested. Wearing a suit and tie looks even more impressive when your competition isn't wearing them, they told me. They also cautioned me to coach my employees about those same values, especially as the company grew bigger. "Put your values down in an employee handbook," they told me. "Sometimes people need to see something in writing in order for them to really get it." And I did: ISI's handbook is modeled after the BBB version, which my father and brother co-authored. And perhaps their biggest gift to me was their willingness to listen to my latest challenge or predicament. I learned some of my most valuable lessons about counting pennies from them, for example, because not only had they both seen countless examples of businesses ruined by careless spending, my brother was able to describe for me his own experiences as a small business owner.

Losing John, in particular, just as ISI was taking off, was devastating for me because when I started ISI, it was something we really came to bond over: he was such a big part of its success. Part of what made his advice so valuable was that it came from his having learned lessons from his hard times. And, to avoid making the same mistakes as he did, John said that four people I should never skimp on were a banker, a lawyer, an accountant and an insurance broker. He told me that the hardest thing for a small business owner to see is that their company will get bigger and you need to plan ahead of time for when that day comes. "I know it might seem hard to justify paying good money to these fellas when you don't have much yourself," he told me. "But believe me, it will be worth it." And he was right: I continue to work with three of the original four guys (we changed accountants- more on that later) for the past 11 years and I don't regret a single penny I ever gave any of them. I have often leaned on them for advice during bad times like the partnership divorce and the embezzlement and they have paid back my investment in them tenfold.

Another of the most critical lessons that John taught me was to reach out to other people. Starting a business can often feel like the loneliest job in the world, but it doesn't have to be. "You're in the fight of your life and you need to work hard to keep it going," he told me. "But you don't have to be a martyr, there are a lot of resources out there if you're willing to ask for help." Using that advice, I have found friends and con-fidantes in so many places, most of them close to home.

After I had moved back to Memphis and started working for ATS, I met Charlie Auerbach, a transplant from Brooklyn, New York, who worked for a financial planning company. Charlie, who worked for the IRS and a few firms on Wall Street before moving to Memphis, started working to help Maureen and me plan for a few ways to save some money for the kid's college funds. But our discussions also evolved into talks about the future of video conferencing and how ATS wasn't doing enough to position itself for that future. Charlie and I would take entire afternoons mapping out plans on the whiteboard in his office; Charlie, in fact, helped me put together a proposal to split out a new division at ATS that I could run. While it was still in its infancy, Charlie saw the potential of the industry – and recognized how profitable it could be. He knew that I was trailblazing a new industry – and that it would be both difficult and expensive to educate most folks about its potential. That's also why, when I said my goodbyes with ATS, Charlie continued to lend me sound advice on how to get started on my own. Charlie, who by then had started his own business, Wealth Strategies Group, Inc., out in Cordova, Tennessee, even introduced me to some preliminary investors that he knew. He also cautioned me that getting startup capital is the hardest kind of money to come by in the world and that I needed to keep pushing if I wanted to land any. While I didn't raise any money through those particular moneymen, I did get the experience of pitching my idea to investors, practice that eventually did pay off as discussed in Chapter 2.

Charlie, I'm lucky to report, continues to lend me invaluable advice, both as a financial confidant but also as a fellow entrepreneur who shares many of the same challenges in running a business as I do. Charlie was one of the first people I asked to join my advisory board – a favor that he has recently returned as I have joined his board. He has also begun to work with me on thinking more about a holistic approach to my business and personal financial portfolio. In other words, how Maureen and I, in part, can take some risk off the table with the business, which is our most valuable asset by far. While I have absolutely no desire to sell the business, we should at least have options like going public or bringing in outside investors on the table, Charlie tells us, because those are ways that we can take some of our personal chips out of the game. Taking a longer view of the business and of your personal financial situation is not something all entrepreneurs excel at, and I'm no exception. That's why I rely so heavily on Charlie's counsel both personally and professionally.

Another one of the key things that I have learned after 11 years in business is you can never be an expert on everything and I have found the best way to learn about being a better small businessman is to always be a good listener and take notes. I might not always take someone's advice, but I will hear them out. I learned about how to negotiate credit arrangements with suppliers from Dr. Barry Gilmore, who taught me both at the University of Memphis and again through the Kauffman Foundation FastTrac program. He reminded me that vendors valued my business as much as I valued theirs and that they have a vested interest in my success. On the other hand, Dr. John Pepin, who also taught me

# Secret Weapons

business at the University of Memphis back in the 1970s, and is now a dean at the university, cautioned me to not rely on any single vendor and to create a single identity of our own. I remember him telling me, "Be careful of the vendors cutting you out as a middle man." That was critical advice that we are working towards even today.

And you can pick up a lot of advice by attending trade shows, dinners or even just having a few drinks with other people in your industry. And that goes for award conferences like the Inc. 500 as well: what better place to pick up a few tips than on the golf course, in a classroom or even the bar with some of the most successful business people out there.

I also have a secret weapon that none of my competitors can match: my wife Maureen. And I tell you what, as any married entrepreneur can tell you, the most valuable unpaid consultant you have is your spouse. You might have the most valuable consultant you'll ever find living under the same roof and never realize it. But if you don't have your spouse in your corner, you're really on your own. If you run your own business, it is so essential to have someone back at home to bounce ideas off of and to give you some good, hard honest answers about them. Not only is Maureen intelligent and street-wise, she has her own background in sales and marketing. She's also a lot more sensitive than me; she plays the right side of my brain and keeps in tune with my employees' feelings. She's extremely good at reading people and that has paid off for ISI more times than I can count with decisions about things like potential hires, new suppliers, and even customer issues.

And while there is a practical side to getting your spouse engaged in the business – spouses usually need to sign a lot of paperwork, especially where loans are involved and, if you incorporate as an S-Corp or a C-Corp, the IRS will come sniffing. Getting a loan to start your business also usually involves putting a second mortgage or even a third on your home – it's not for the faint of heart. But it's a lot more than just the paperwork that's at risk. In my experience, 99 percent of the entrepreneurs that I know that didn't make it didn't get their spouse involved in the business or have his or her support. Your spouse has to believe that you can get it done, and I know that there were some days that I would never have made it out of bed if it weren't for Maureen. If I haven't said it enough Maureen: I love you.

# Secret Weapons

*December 8, 1996 - Dad turns 80 - I turn 40 - Dad always knew what advice I needed about ISI and when to give it.*

*John and me in 2001 — I never made an important decision concerning ISI without John's input.*

# Keep *Swinging*

*The Budding Entrepreneur meets the Legend- Meeting the man that started Holiday Inns was a thrilling moment for me in 1996.*

# Chapter Six

# THE COMEBACK

*Surviving the Day My Business Almost Died*

*April 30, 2003*

The morning after the worst day of my life, Maureen helped drag me out of bed to meet up with my friend Andy at the office. He was going to try and find out how much damage Linda has done. He warned me that it wasn't going to be pretty. He was right – it was ugly. Real ugly.

We spent the next several days buried in the books, fueled by coffee and fast food. Linda was a pro. She burrowed her way into my computer system like a virus. She set herself up as a vendor in the accounts payable system. There was a rubber stamp with my signature, forged. My name - her handwriting. She had been cutting checks to herself. A lot of them. For almost one year. As we kept digging and untangling, the damage continued to mount, a $1,500 commission here, a $10,000 check there – $257,379 in total. I always wondered how she afforded the slick clothes, the gold and diamonds, the trip to Disney World where she stayed at the Grand Floridian. Hell, I couldn't even afford to take my family there. My anger, however, was swiftly replaced by fear. The business was growing, providing for 16 families, but I, we, couldn't afford to lose $257,379. That's four or five salaries, two years of rent and a few

# Keep *Swinging*

Christmas bonuses. Thank God we had almost $75,000 coming from a Fidelity bond – an insurance policy of sorts that compensates businesses for an employee's negligent or dishonest behavior. It would help, but would it be enough?

I hit a new low later that week. I was driving my teenage daughter to basketball practice and I asked her how she was doing. "How's school?"

Everything was fine, she said, but she wanted to ask me a question. "Fire away," I said. "Daddy, are we going to lose our house because that woman stole from you," she asked? I took a second to gather my thoughts. "I hope not honey," I said, "but I really don't know how everything is going to turn out." The look on her face broke my heart.

I thought back to what could have driven Linda to do this to me. She always seemed to resent the money the company made, the money I made, the fact that my wife and kids got paid for work they did for us. She always made comments about how my sales force was overpaid. She talked about how she always wanted a Lexus, that she was entitled to it. Maybe she thought I was just too juicy a target to resist.

A few days later I caught a break. At church that Sunday, I ran into a friend, Rick Harlow. He's the special agent in charge with the Memphis Secret Service. I remembered that Secret Service agents not only act as bodyguards for the president of the United States, they also

# The Comeback

investigate counterfeiting, fraud and embezzlement cases. He told me to take a deep breath and calm down. He'd take it from here. I actually hugged him, squeezing him hard. I wasn't in this alone anymore, I thought. That night, for the first time in a long time, I slept straight through to the morning.

Patrick Davis, an agent that works for Rick, showed up at 8:30 a.m. on Monday with some interesting news. While I knew from Andy that Linda had been involved in some kind of embezzlement before, Patrick told me that she had done this exact same scam at least three other times. We never checked for any civil lawsuits brought against her, the kind that would be filed to recoup losses, but her other employers didn't give us reason to. Turns out, according to Davis, she admitted to stealing more than $2 million on her last job. The company buried the story, kept it quiet (sort of). They were in fact pursuing Linda through the civil courts where they hoped to get some money back from her. Now I'm thinking, that's why we didn't find out anything about Linda's past thefts when we did a background check. We only checked criminal records. I guess I should consider myself lucky. We caught her early.

I had a decision to make, however. Do I go after Linda - do I prosecute her? Most small business owners wouldn't. It's too expensive and too distracting, they say. Bad publicity. The courts will let her go with a slap on the wrist anyway. Besides, she's probably already spent the money. We'll be lucky to get anything back from her. Maybe it's best to pretend it never happened, I wondered, just cover it up and start over.

No. John would do the right thing. He and my dad ran the Memphis area Better Business Bureau for almost 40 years. I could hear them whispering in my ear. I needed to see this through, for them, for me. It is the way I was raised, justice. I'm an Eagle Scout, after all. I needed to send that woman to jail even if I never got a cent from her. I needed to make a lesson out of myself. It was the right thing to do, I said. I set my jaw and continued the pursuit.

Two days later, Linda still wasn't returning our calls. I drove to her house, knocked on the door, hard. No answer. We kept calling on the phone, leaving message after message. Finally, she picked up. "Linda, we need to talk about these bonuses", I said. "Not now," she replied. "I'll call back in an hour." The next call we got, however, was from her attorney. Even though she was still an employee, Linda's lawyer had advised her not to talk to us. "And you'll be hearing further from me about Linda's daughter Angela as well," he said. I think my heart stopped for a split second. "Hold on," I say in a low, slow voice. "Did you just say that Angela is Linda's daughter?" While the lawyer tried to talk his way around his mistake, the train was already out of the station. My anger burns anew: Linda had the gall to hire her own daughter without telling anyone! And they worked together to steal from me! No wonder that

# The Comeback

when we searched through Linda's office for evidence, we all noticed something strange: there were no pictures anywhere. While we thought it was weird, we really didn't think much of it at the time. Now it all makes sense: if she had any pictures of her daughter and her grandchildren, we would have made the connection that Angela was Linda's daughter. While many daughters share at least some resemblance to their mothers – Angela and Linda looked nothing alike. But maybe one of Angela's children did, and Linda was clearly paranoid enough not to risk having a picture in her office to prove it. It was almost too unbelievable to be true. Not only did this justify the decision to fire Angela, it also made it clear what I had to do next. If we couldn't track down Linda in person, we would do the next best thing: We ended up firing her by certified mail one week later, May 6, 2003.

Meanwhile, with black-suited agents coming and going, the rest of my employees knew something was wrong. They knew it involved Linda and Angela, but the rumor mill was churning overtime. They tiptoed around the office. They avoided me whenever possible. They were worried that they would be let go, that the company would go bankrupt. They were probably already looking for new jobs. I recognized the need to do something, so I drafted a letter to each of them and their families.

# Keep *Swinging*

I didn't know how they would take it and I hoped they would all decide to stay. I needed them.

*Dear John and Marie:*

*I am writing this letter to all employees of Interactive Solutions with reference to the recent crisis involving two of our employees, Linda Merritt and Angela Bell...*

*I detailed the facts: the unwarranted bonuses, the forged checks and the history of embezzlement. I told them the company was strong and profitable and we had help. The secret service was on the case as well as our accounting firm and Andy Wilson. We had a $75,000 insurance policy to cover part of the loss. I told them that we also had ZERO tolerance for dishonesty or theft in our company. We were going to pursue prosecution of Linda and Angela - no matter how long it took.*

*I appreciate your hard work and support in these trying days and please continue to keep the company in your thoughts and prayers.*

*Sincerely,*

Jay B. Myers

A day later, I was thrilled to find that my fears were unfounded. The letters broke down the walls. Everyone felt wronged by Linda and

# The Comeback

Angela, and they were taking it personally. We are going to keep motoring on towards our goals for the year, they said. We started a cost-cutting campaign using a chart that looks like one used to track the results of a blood drive. When someone saved $139 on recycled office paper, we moved up the chart an inch. When someone else saved almost a thousand dollars by adding another leg to their flight, we moved up six inches. We even decided to have a company outing at the local ballpark - home of the Triple A Memphis Redbirds - for what Maureen called an ole-fashioned "throw down." Someone even made up t-shirts for it printed with "I Survived 4/29/03" on them. I was relieved: We were going to take this on as a team. That's when I learned that I had some tough people working for me.

It didn't stop there either. In November, the local Memphis newspaper, The Commercial Appeal, ran the whole story, warts and all. News spread quickly throughout Memphis and the calls and letters starting pouring in. We're praying for you, they wrote. You are an inspiration, they said. We need to see more of your determination, conviction, and moral courage in today's society. Hang in there. Thank you, we will, we said.

Eventually, the Secret Service had enough information in July 2003 using our case and the three others to pick up Linda, again. She had posted $20,000 for bail the last time, but couldn't escape the feds twice. It was September 2003. They cuffed her and brought her to jail, first to the federal prison in Memphis and eventually to its counterpart in Mason, Tennessee. Turns out she had landed a job working for another company in between her stints in jail. I know because the owner of the company called me to ask about her. Apparently she had borrowed money from the company and the owner had confronted her about it. He had called me to find out if she had done something similar with me. I filled him in about what had happened to me and – literally as we were on the phone – he said that Linda had just peeled out of his parking lot with a handful of checks. Though she worked there for just two weeks, Linda was accused of stealing $4,000 from them. I felt so vindicated in my decision to push forward in prosecuting her. I never wanted to see this ever happen again.

Meanwhile, we continued to build our case against her. We had our proof of loss from the insurance company and the evidence was strong. Just as we feared, most of the money was gone, but the Secret Service recovered five pieces of gold, silver and diamond jewelry from Linda's home worth about $25,000. Of course, Linda had a long list of creditors waiting for their fair share as well. We agreed to take a percentage of that while the government took the rest to cover its costs in prosecuting the case against Linda.

# The Comeback

The court system, however, was frustrating and slow. She kept getting trial dates delayed. Linda had a million excuses, illnesses and back problems caused by living in her cell. Luckily, we had Tracy Berry, the Assistant U.S. attorney, going to bat for us. She kept pushing.

Finally, on March 16, 2004, the first victory: A hearing, held in a downtown courtroom. Linda plead guilty to two counts of bank fraud. Sentencing, however, was delayed until September.

In the months in between the hearing and the expected sentencing, I tried to act normal again, to start focusing on growing the business in a way that I hadn't in some time. The experience had taught me how important the success of the company was to my wellbeing – and to my employees as well. The trauma of the past few months, in a way, had brought us closer together as a team, given us a common enemy to overcome. Now, we needed to get past it the best we could. We had sales to make. Ironically enough, despite all of the turmoil of 2003, the company smashed our sales records in 2004 - doubling total revenue to over $10 million.

I couldn't say I forgot about Linda and all that she had wrought while we waited for the sentencing. I thought about it, her, a lot. But the pain was gradually receding under the rigors of the job, of my family. My kids were getting older, and bringing an entirely different set of worries back home with them. The company continued to grow like crazy, and we had been able to weather the storm and cash shortfall rather well.

For her part, Linda was apparently having a rough go of jail. She was behind bars in a federal prison in Texas. Tracy and Rick would report in to me that Linda was sick or injured most of the time. They were worried that Linda might be able to postpone the sentencing. Rather than September, it was looking like it would be pushed a few more months. I grew very frustrated – I just wanted it to end, one way or another.

Finally, in November 2004, we got a call from the Justice Department. They had given me a victim identification number – 663482 – and the call said that the sentencing hearing had been set: November 22nd would be the day. Unfortunately, my 84-year-old mother had passed away just 17 days earlier after a long illness and I was still feeling the pain. But I knew I needed to do this, to set the pain aside and get this done for Mom, Dad and John, I told myself. So with Maureen in tow, we entered the Federal courthouse and quietly took our seats at the back of the courtroom.

Then, it was my turn to take the stand. I won't lie: I was nervous. After all this time, I didn't know what I was going to feel. Looking at Tracy helps, I just focus on her eyes and on making out the words to her questions about Linda. My chest puffs out and my eyes go red. It is cathartic.

# The Comeback

I start talking fast, about how sick Linda is, how her dishonesty and terrible behavior put my employees and our livelihoods at risk. I list off what I found out about her. About how she lied to us about Angela, lied to us about her past, lied to me when I hired her. Judge, I say, I plead with you to put this woman away for as long as you possibly can. The judge nods, thanks me and asks me to step down. With that, I deflate and trudge back to my seat, nearly exhausted.

Back in my seat, the judge looks too calm. She's going to let Linda off, I think. All of this will be a waste. I start to shake again. Maureen whispers over to me – you hit a home run, she says.

The judge speaks. She says - her eyes locked onto Linda – she originally intended to hand down a sentence of 60 months. But, after hearing my pleas, she was sentencing Linda to the maximum of 100 months. All of us - Me, Maureen, Tracy – erupt with hollers of joy as I high-five the attorney and the secret service agent. Justice has prevailed.

The amazing thing, however, is that after the judge announces the sentence, Linda turns to Maureen and me and says, "I'm sorry - I never meant to hurt you." I turn away, put my arm around Maureen, stand up and walk out of the courtroom with a smile on my face.

# Keep *Swinging*

Today, Linda remains in prison in Texas. She's due to be released on October 10, 2010. She isn't eligible for parole. The Secret Service has since advised me that it is unlikely that I will ever receive any money from her. Her list of creditors is just too long. Angela Bell, on the other hand, continues to send me certified checks for $200 every month to pay back the $4,500 she stole. As I understand it she was able to work out a plea arrangement with the government as part of their diversion program. Unbelievably, I actually ran into Angela last year at a Memphis Grizzlies game. She came up to me and my family, smiled, and asked how we were doing. I think I mumbled something to the effect that we were doing fine. I still am shocked she had the guts to approach me.

I am often asked if I could forgive these two women. They put me through the most gut-wrenching 10 months of my life. As a man of faith, I'd like to say I could, at least for their children and grandchildren's sake. Part of me will always want to see them both pay their debts to God for what they did and because they did it coming on the heels of my brother's death.

In an effort to learn from the past (and do some research for this book), about two years or so after the judge sent Linda to jail, I paid Rick Harlow a visit in his office in East Memphis. Since I see him just about every Sunday at church, Rick has really been someone I could lean on

# The Comeback

as I tried to bury the past and focus on the future. When I see Rick at church with his family in tow, I sometimes forget whom he works for: he is just so friendly. (For his part, Rick told me that when he saw me on the day I found out about Linda, he said I had all the classic signs of a heart attack victim: ashen face, sweaty palms and shaking.) But when I walked into his office to talk to him about Linda, he was actually on the phone discussing an order for some shotguns. And after seeing Rick shaking hands with the first President Bush along with a series of other photographs of Presidents Clinton, Reagan, Ford, Nixon – along with one of Pope John Paul II – I was in awe.

Rick's office was instrumental in making the case against Linda, which seems like a strange task for the Secret Service. But, as Rick explained to me, the Secret Service was actually started in 1865 to fight counterfeiting since, in the wake of the Civil War, more than one-third of the currency circulating at that time was counterfeit. That made the service, Rick explained, one of the first federal investigative agencies. Agents working for the Service didn't take on protecting the president until after President McKinley's assassination in 1901. And while most folks might assume that the FBI would take on a case like mine, they'd be wrong, Rick told me and, by the way, nine transplanted members of the Secret Service formed the FBI in 1908. When you have trouble with money, Rick insisted, companies should call him up ASAP.

# Keep *Swinging*

Rick, who moved to Memphis from Washington D.C. in 2000, told me that Memphis is the personal bankruptcy capital of the world, and that means that many, many businesses are at risk of employee fraud and embezzlement. When an employee is facing dire financial circumstances, it becomes easier for them to justify stealing from their employer, Rick explained to me, a trend that is exploding with all the information now available on computers and the Internet. The U.S. Chamber of Commerce, in fact, estimates that employers lose between $20 billion and $40 billion each and every year to employee theft. That's billion with a b. I guess $257,000 isn't so bad in comparison. And Rick told me that I was a classic victim: in mourning over John's death, I had relaxed the controls in the business – losing track of the bank statements - and Linda was there, ready to take advantage. "Companies can eliminate 99 percent of the risk of fraud if they simply follow their own set of checks and balances," Rick told me. "As soon as someone gets too comfortable with their employees, maybe trusts them too much and lets those rules lax, the wrong kind of person will manipulate that sense of security."

But I sure wasn't alone in falling prey to someone. In his experience, Rick told me that it is often women who make the best embezzler because their employers tend to trust them more. The most common kind of case he gets called in on usually involves, ironically, a church administrator. But there was also the case of a local Memphis bank and its longtime vault manager. This bank was apparently a banker's bank,

# The Comeback

meaning their vaults held about $6 million of other bank's deposits at any one time. Well, as Rick explained it, the vault's manager was a 60-year-old woman who had been working there forever. And because she had been there so long, she had been able to avoid any scrutiny, or audits, for some time – that is until just last year when she took a vacation and the bank ran a vault audit. It was only then that they discovered about $895,000 missing. Turns out that that manager may have gotten wind of something because she and her husband disappeared, abandoning most of their Memphis possessions, including their home. She might have gotten away with it too if not for that fact that this manager's husband had kept his stock trading account open and, after securing a subpoena to get the internet IP address that was connecting to the account, Rick's team tracked down the couple in a Florida hotel room. The lesson learned, Rick told me, was that no employee should be considered above reproach if their job involves handling a company's funds – while they might start small, just a one-time withdrawal to cover the mortgage or the rent, it only snowballs from there. "The best way to prevent the kind of thing that happened to you is to take away the opportunity," he told me.

As depressing as Rick's stories and advice were, it brought home an important point for me: not only was I lucky to not have been hit worse, I did the right thing by going public with what had happened. Many companies, especially public companies or, worse still, banks, figure they can ill afford the confidence hit they would experience if they admitted they had been robbed by an employee. That also means that whenever I ask my friend Andy Wilson, the fraud examiner who also helped me put Linda behind bars, how business is going, and he says great, that means another company like mine has taken a hit. And professionals like Andy, though not cheap, are worth every penny for their help.

In thinking about what I had learned from the experience, I feel like it all happened for a reason. The experience has changed me, has changed the way I run my business. We now do background checks on all new employees: both criminal and civil. I use my lunch breaks to deposit all of our checks at a bank around the corner from the office. I know I trust people less than I used to. I have also learned a lot about my employees and myself. I learned not to bury my head in the sand when disaster strikes, hoping it would all go away. And finally, I learned about character and the need to take action and to stand up for what you believe in, both in your personal and professional life. Sometimes the right thing to do isn't always the easiest. It's a set of lessons I will not soon forget.

# The Comeback

*We Survived 4-29-03 (Left to Right) Andrew Ruhland, John DeLockery, Me, Kevin Carmon, Annelle Hochhauser, Troy Holden and Linda Godsey- The embezzlement crisis taught us a lot about business and ourselves.*

# Chapter Seven

# CREATIVE RECRUITING & RETENTION
*How to recruit and keep your best people*


Don Cottam's first day working for ISI back in 1997 sure was a doozy: he started the exact day my partner and I ended our business relationship. The first task I gave him was to drive out to my now ex-partner's office in Murray, Kentucky, pack up any equipment that belonged to the company, and truck it back to our offices in Memphis. If I hadn't known Don better, I might have guessed he wouldn't have shown up the next day. Who wants to wade into a business divorce on their first day? I knew he was a tough cookie, though, I chose to send him for a reason: I knew I could trust him.

Maureen and I had met Don a few years before that day: he was a waiter at the Pub on the Pike, our version of Cheers, where we met up most Friday nights to have dinner with friends. Everyone loved Don, who was a student at the University of Memphis at the time - he was a high-energy guy that was easy to talk to. One such Friday night, as Maureen and I sat around chatting with a bunch of our friends, Ken Forbes, one of my oldest pals, pulled me aside and pointed out Don, who was darting all over the place, taking orders, bringing food and, no matter how busy things got, he never stopped smiling. "You know, if I owned a business,

# Keep *Swinging*

I would look at hiring that kid," he told me. "He has hustle." And, while ISI wasn't ready to hire any new fulltime employees, I kept that piece of advice Ken gave me tucked away.

Then, in 1997, I was finally ready to expand the sales force beyond its sole rainmaker, namely me. So I decided to see where that kid Don had moved on to. Turns out that after a brief stint working at the Half Shell, another restaurant in town, Don was over in Arkansas working for a company building furniture. I drove out to meet him, and over lunch, I learned that while he didn't have any sales experience, he had run his own computer repair business when he was in college. I knew that if I hired his hustle, selling was going to come naturally – especially since he wasn't going to be intimidated by the technology, or putting in long hours. This guy was a worker and that's what I needed – I could teach him the rest. I didn't need to know any more than that: I offered him a job on the spot. He accepted and, after serving out his two-week notice, he headed out to Murray to help launch the rebirth of ISI.

The reason I sent Don on what might have seemed like a suicide mission of sorts was that Don had served my partner food and drinks many times on his visits to Memphis, and I knew Don could pretty much talk his way out of anything. That's partly why I had hired him after all. But I also needed someone who could help mend fences and not burn bridges – despite our troubles I still hoped that my partner and I could

# Creative Recruiting & Retention

salvage something of our friendship. If I had just hired a random moving company or, worse yet, went myself, it might have only added fuel to the fire. It turns out that, in the end, I chose the right man for the job. During our debriefing after he got back from Murray, Don told me it was tense at first: my partner was still feeling pretty burned by the whole experience. But my now ex-partner and he had always been friendly before, so they were able to quickly find some common ground. In fact, before Don headed back to Memphis, the tension had calmed down to the point where my now ex-partner's wife asked him to stay for lunch. Talk about smooth - that would be Don.

Don also proved his ability to think on his feet in other ways as well. A perfect example of this was a few years later, when we had outgrown my original executive suite and had moved into a much larger office on Highway 72 in Collierville. At the time Maureen was working with a local charity that had put together a cookbook that they hoped to sell to raise some money. The problem was that, after they had 10,000 of these books printed up, they had nowhere to store them. We had some space in our warehouse at the time, which was more like an empty office, so I offered it up – not really knowing what I was committing to. When the truck showed up stuffed full with hundreds of boxes, I knew we were in trouble. Our office at the time didn't have a loading dock, so I had to recruit Derek and Don – ISI's original two employees - to help me haul each and every one of those boxes by hand into the back of our office – repeatedly getting up and down out of that truck. I can only imagine how they must have been cussing me under their breath - especially when I took off to make some sales calls and left them to tackle all the work!

It was actually Don, though, who figured out a way to take advantage of the situation. Not long after he and Derek had unloaded those books, Don and I hosted a sales prospect to demonstrate how our video conferencing products work. Derek had wired the entire office with various cameras, so in our demonstrations, we could pan around to show off the system. When Don got to the warehouse room though, he decided to show off a bit as he focused the camera on all of Maureen's boxes: "You can see our warehouse here," Don said without skipping a beat. "And you'll notice all the inventory we have ready to ship out to customers." Inventory? Those were cookbooks! After staring at Don for a second, I shot a glance at the prospect who, actually, seemed impressed. Luckily for us, the image on the screen was fuzzy enough that no one noticed the labels on those boxes. Talk about chutzpah...

Don's been with ISI going on nine years now, evolving from a junior salesman to heading up our satellite office in Nashville, which has grown into a huge part of our business. After a slow start to his sales career, he has now come on like gangbusters: selling more than $20 million worth of equipment in his nine years. I don't quite know

# Creative Recruiting & Retention

where ISI would be today if it weren't for Don – and all the other employees I hired using the exact same criteria – HUSTLE.

One of the biggest challenges for any growing company is finding – and keeping – top-notch employees. All too often, companies, including ISI, have been prone to hiring the wrong people for the wrong reasons, usually because you're crunched in some way. Let me be first in line to say that you need to be recruiting people long before you actually need them, because when you need an extra pair of hands to fulfill that new customer order or to go out on an install, you probably won't have the time to make the best decision. And headhunters are never the answer. The truth is you never know where you might meet a quality person - You would be amazed where I have done my best recruiting. While ISI has seen its share of turnover since we got our start, I have been incredibly fortunate to have attracted a core of people that continue to stick with me through thick and thin, an all-star roster that includes Don; Derek Plummer, my head of engineering and design, was the first employee I hired at ISI 10 years ago; Kevin Carmon, who worked for me at ATS; John DeLockery, a former customer of ours; Andrew Ruhland our VP of Sales who has been with us for six years; and Annelle Hochhauser, who joined us in the wake of the Linda Merritt disaster four years ago. I met each one of these folks in unique ways – because I'm always on the look out for hustle before I ever get to a resume.

My appreciation for a solid work ethic dates back to my childhood in Louisiana, where my mother and father both had jobs to support their growing family, which included five boys and two girls. Because money was tight, and there was just as much work to get done at home, my brothers and sisters and I had a list of chores we had to take care of on a daily basis, even though some of us had part-time jobs of one sort or another. The after-school tasks included all the standard drudgery that most kids have to tackle, everything from washing the dishes to taking out the garbage. But my mom's real pride and joy was her garden, and she kept a close eye on whomever had the job of yanking weeds from among her prized flowers and vegetables, which was usually me. I'll never forget hitting my knees and starting to work in the dirt as my mom backed the car out of the driveway, hollering out, "I want to see your head down and your tail up!"

While I can't admit I completely appreciated the advice at the time, when I would rather have been riding around on my bicycle or skipping stones and catching frogs down by the pond, I learned what hard work meant. That also meant that, even though I was good for mostly Cs in school, I knew that if I worked harder than everyone else, I could accomplish just as much, if not more, than any Ivy Leaguer who was

# Creative Recruiting & Retention

resting on their fancy degree. And don't get me wrong – I value a good education and I am proud that my own kids, Jordan and Katie, are exceptional scholars. But grades aren't enough: they need to be combined with that ability to put your head down and your tail up. So when I went looking for people to work with at ISI, I went looking for hard workers, and no one I have ever met works harder than Derek Plummer.

Derek, if you can believe it, actually lived in Murray, home of my ex-partner, before he joined ISI. I first met Derek when he was still a student at Murray State University. And what impressed me most was that he didn't just go to school, he worked at the Briggs & Stratton factory in town building engines, balancing his school work with some needed overtime. Derek had always been a worker and survivor, but he also happened to be the best darn electrical engineering student Murray State had churned out in some time. While he didn't know a lick about video conferencing, nobody did – the technology was still in its infancy, and that really got Derek excited. He is the type of guy who when he wants to get something done, he makes it a competition: he puts his head down and goes. My partner and I, of course, loved his potential and offered him a job, part-time at first until he finished school. Then, after he graduated in May 1997, Derek, who was newly married at the time, agreed to move to Memphis and start work as ISI's first fulltime employee. I always chuckle when Derek talks about what a conservative person he is and how much he dislikes risk: how many 22-year old newlyweds do you know that would be willing to up and move to work for a company that sold technology that hardly anybody had ever heard of, let alone one where its two owners had just split up?

And having the courage to take a few risks is another bond we all share at ISI. I reconnected with Kevin Carmon, who was a crack technician back at ATS, completely by accident. I ran into his wife one day at the Methodist Hospital, where, she told me, Kevin had taken a job as a data entry clerk after leaving ATS. I knew Kevin was my kind of guy – I remembered that he had worked at an ice house at one time in his life and what job could be harder than hauling ice around all day? Talk about hustle! So I asked both he and his wife out to lunch, told them what I could offer, which was a lot more risk than working at a hospital would be, but a lot more freedom to create something to be proud of. Spurred on by the huge smile his wife was wearing, Kevin accepted my offer on the spot.

Another guy that I had an easy time convincing to join our ship was John DeLockery, who is now our Vice President of Operations. John was actually our liaison at one of our early customers, Alpha Corporation in Collierville. When Alpha changed gears seven years ago, however, deciding they didn't need someone with John's experience in technolo-

# Creative Recruiting & Retention

gy, I swooped in and offered him a chance to work for ISI as a contractor, helping us with our installations in the field: and he was a perfect fit. As we flew him around the country, from Oak Ridge, Tennessee, to Silicon Valley, California, John's experience installing the equipment for Alpha gave him a head start in learning on the fly for ISI. It took a special person to adapt to the new products we were bringing in, and John had the ideal personality to deal with both problem solving and making the customer feel like we would do whatever we needed to do to get the job done.

In 2001, a year after I hired John, I was looking to fill yet another position – specifically another salesperson to augment Don and myself. This time, I called up a marketing professor at the University of Memphis, Walt Drissel, and asked him who the hotshot student was that year in his sales and marketing class. Walt was the chair of the department and, about two seconds after I asked him, he told me – "Give Andrew Ruhland a call." Andrew, it turned out, had moved after graduation from the U of M to work for a telecom company in Little Rock, Arkansas. I again hopped in my car and made the two-hour drive to buy Andrew some lunch and see if I could convince him to move back to Memphis. And, after I heard his stories about paying his way through school driving a seafood truck up and down the coast on weekends and summers while pulling double shifts at restaurants and bars at night, I knew I had my man.

# Keep *Swinging*

And, lest you think that I have used my creative recruiting methods on just men, I met my chief financial officer Annelle Hochhauser under less than favorable conditions. But that is where she proved her character to me. Annelle was actually employed by the accounting firm that had failed to identify any wrongdoing in ISI's books on the part of Linda Merritt. Annelle was part of the team the company sent to ISI in the wake of my discovery and she, to her credit, told me that her firm had blown it. I remember really appreciating that she said that. In response, I think I may have muttered something to the effect of, "Do you know of anyone that would be interested in taking an accounting manager position with us?" After a pause, she said, "Well I can't solicit jobs from our customers, but I would be interested." Well, the short story is that Annelle quit her job at that accounting firm, without any guarantee from me, and soon thereafter, I did in fact hire her to help sort out ISI's affairs and she has been a blessing ever since.

Annelle's story shows that, like I said earlier, you always have to be on the lookout for talented people, no matter when or where you might come across them. My most recent example dates back to last year when I was again looking to add to ISI's sales team. One night over dinner, I was complaining to Maureen about how hard it was to find someone worth their salt. I might even be forced to consider calling up a head-hunter, I said with a sigh. "How about Jeremy Johnson?" she asked. Yeah, how about Jeremy Johnson! Maureen, as usual, came to my rescue.

# Creative Recruiting & Retention

Jeremy had at one time worked for our local dry cleaners, so we both used to run into him every week or two. I remember how energetic he was – no matter how hot and humid it was - how I never once had a lost piece of clothing when Jeremy was working and how much fun I had talking about Memphis basketball with him. And, as Maureen pointed out, he always remembered everybody's name – always greeting us with a "Good morning Mr. or Mrs. Myers." While it might seem like a common sense or insignificant skill, it isn't – you can't teach that – and it is a critical skill for any successful salesperson to have in their arsenal. After Maureen's revelation, I tracked Jeremy down at his latest venture: he had taken a job selling DHL services in town, where he was on track to be their top salesman that year. Consider that: the fact that this guy could sell DHL services in FedEx's hometown was worth more than any college degree. And, after another one of my now famous lunches, this time at a Subway in Brownsville, Tennessee, I offered Jeremy a job, and he accepted. Again, with Jeremy, I hired the hustle, and doing that hasn't let me down yet.

## *Retaining: Just As Critical as Recruiting*

As important as it is to be on the lookout for potential new employees, it is even more critical to take care of the employees you already have: it can be particularly devastating to a young business when a key employee or employees leave the company, especially when you invest years of time and effort in training them in a specialized skill like video conferencing technology. There have also been numerous times when other firms and competitors have tried to recruit our top folks – trying to lure them away with the promise of working for a bigger and better company. That's why we at ISI work so hard to create the kind of business environment that not only are we all proud to be a part of, but takes care of everyone's pocketbook as well. In the end, if an employee leaves just because he or she simply wants more money, we probably didn't need them anyway.

The funny thing that I've learned as a CEO, though, is that even if you offer your employees great health care benefits, a 401(k) plan and even profit sharing, what the best employees really want is a job at an honest company that they can be proud of. When they meet up with friends and family, they don't want to have to apologize for working for so-and-so Inc. – they want to brag about all the neat things their company is up to. They of course want to be compensated well, but any company that encourages its employees to chase dollar signs before everything else is doomed in my opinion. Fortunately, I have learned that even a smaller business can retain its best employees if it aims to be more than just any old company.

# Creative Recruiting & Retention

## *Aim High...*

When ISI was three years old, I submitted an application to be considered for the small business of the year as determined by the Memphis Business Journal. And that application was thorough: they asked you for three year's worth of financial information, conducted on-site interviews of me and my staff, obtained customer and professional references and even discussed what kinds of things that we had done to give back to the community. So why did I go through all that just for the chance to win some award?

I'll admit a certain amount of it was about stroking my ego. But more importantly, I did it to give the business something to shoot for. We're real big on corporate recognition. You can't afford to just float around. You need to have goals to drive the business and motivate the troops. It also worked like a report card of sorts, a good self-examination to see where we were. People from all parts of the company got involved in completing that application and it gave them a sense of pride, it made them feel good about the business they were working for, whether we won or not.

# Keep *Swinging*

Applying for awards like that one from the Memphis Business Journal is a real motivator for the people in the organization. When people feel good about what their business has accomplished, and even better about where it is going, they will want to stick around and see how it all turns out. It is a chance for your top-performers to get some recognition for their efforts – to take a bow in front of their peers. Even if you don't win, you get a ton of free publicity. Some 65,000 people in the community read the MBJ alone. That, of course, also helps with recruiting, as people want to work for companies that are headed somewhere. It is also a great way to reinforce relationships with key customers and suppliers who appreciate dealing with a company they perceive as a "winner."

In 2000, ISI was chosen as a finalist for the Small Business of the Year. We bought a bunch of tables for the awards dinner and invited the employees and their spouses. Even though we didn't win, it was still a celebration. It was so cool and fun to be recognized by our local business community. When ISI really turned the corner the following year, we not only won the 2001 Small Business of the Year award, but also made the Inc. 500, ranking as the 182nd fastest-growing private company in the country, which for me personally, was a great honor. For the Inc. 500 award, we really went all out to use the recognition as a motivator to show that ISI was really on the move. Before winning that award, ISI was thought of as a local company doing some pretty neat things with video technology, but mostly as just a Tennessee company with local

# Creative Recruiting & Retention

customers. After winning the Inc. 500 award, however, we suddenly felt like we were among the elite small businesses in the country. Now, we could do business just about anywhere. We even hosted a formal reception in recognition of our accomplishment, inviting employees and their spouses, key customers, suppliers and other friends of the firm. We included everyone that dealt with us in on the celebration so they could be excited about our success and the future of ISI, and that was the key accomplishment of the event. Earning recognition through business awards like the Inc. 500 are a great opportunity to bring your customers, employees and suppliers together to form a potent combination of people interested in your company's success. People love to be around a company that is eager to share its success with the people and companies that helped them get there.

But we didn't stop there. We were named by Business Tennessee Magazine as one of the fastest growing firms in the state and even made the Inc. 500 again in 2003, at no. 410. We were also recognized with awards from one of our suppliers, Tandberg, and from the Oak Ridge National Laboratories, which we earned on the basis of completing our contract on time and on budget (what a novel concept in government work!). The funny thing about this award was that I had gone to visit the Oak Ridge office on the afternoon before they officially announced that we had won the award. I was given a personal tour of the visitor's center, where we had installed a bunch of neat AV/Video conferencing equipment throughout the center's 10 high-tech conference rooms. During a stop on the tour, I looked out the window and noticed a bunch of people standing around in the middle of the partly paved parking lot. They looked kind of confused and disorganized. My tour guide noticed what I was looking at and shot me a disgusted look. "Can I let you in on a secret?" she asked. "That firm out there doing the paving is over-budget and about 6 months behind schedule. I can tell you that they will not be getting an award from us tomorrow. I still chuckle a bit when I think that we actually won an award for doing what we said we were going to do. It must be an old-fashioned sentiment in these days and times.

Probably the award I am most proud of is when we won the first ever Kemmons Wilson Emerging Business award in 2003, named for my hero and unpaid consultant. The awards luncheon was a big affair, as the entire Memphis business community showed up. The event doubled as the Memphis Regional Chamber of Commerce's Annual Luncheon and there must have been about 1,000 people that turned out at the Memphis Racquet Club banquet hall that day. It was a true honor to walk to the podium after they announced ISI as the winner of the award. As I made that walk, amidst a lot of welcome applause, I couldn't help but remember what a complete nightmare 2003 had been for both the company and me. We were lucky just to survive, let alone earn a prestigious business award. But, as I stood at the podium and looked out at all those smiling faces, all the bad stuff went away: I just

# Creative Recruiting & Retention

felt so proud to be receiving an award on behalf of everyone at ISI, particularly an award named for Mr. Wilson. Unlike the Inc. 500, which rewards revenue growth exclusively, we earned the Emerging Business Award because of the way we value our employees and partners, how we manage for innovation and that we promote corporate values and good citizenship both in the workplace and in the community. In short, all the things that I want ISI to stand for. To make the moment even sweeter, the guest speaker that day was Jerry West, the NBA Hall-of-Famer and general manager of my hometown Grizzlies. Because I am a sports nut, and after all the struggles we had experienced in 2003, receiving such a prestigious award from no less a legend than Jerry West is a moment I will never forget.

## ...But Don't Overlook the Little Things

As important as striving for awards is, you can't forget to take care of your employees in smaller ways as well. One way we do that is by encouraging a family-style environment around the office. I encourage people to bring their family into the office – and to leave the office to take care of their family and themselves. Derek, my head of engineering, for example, is an absolute workaholic who was putting in late hours seven days a week. I think he got to a point where he was headed for some kind of serious burnout. And his wife was no better – she tried to encourage him to find some balance and she came to me for help. So, when it came time for Derek's performance review, I told him he was going to be measured on how well he put some balance back into his life with his wife. And it worked: Derek started backing off the hours some, staffed up his department to handle more of the load, and even started taking a couple of vacations with his wife. Derek and his wife Jennifer, I am proud to report, are now the parents of a beautiful baby girl named Aubrey. The thing is I know Derek was killing himself to help the business. If I had overlooked that, I would have eventually lost not only a top-performing employee, but also a member of my family. Derek got into trouble because of the business, and like any of my family members, I wanted to help him out of it.

And acting like a family isn't always about bailing each other out of trouble either: it's about having some fun too. Everyone gets a card and a cake on their birthday and we typically do a summer event where all the employees and their families head out to see a Memphis Red Birds baseball game, complete with plenty of popcorn and hotdogs. We also make a big deal out of our Christmas party each year since it's a chance to acknowledge all the hard work everyone has done all year. Even when the business wasn't going so good, I always handed out a Christmas bonus, $100 for each month the employee had been with the company. In 2003, because of all the troubles we had been through with Linda

# Creative Recruiting & Retention

Merritt, and despite the theft, I doubled everyone's Christmas bonus as a thank you for sticking with me. I told my employees point blank: "Linda and Angela stole from me, not you, so I won't penalize you for what they did." Does this make me a hero? Of course not – it was simply the right thing to do. And later, to celebrate our second inclusion on the Inc. 500, we did a couple of additional things. First, we held another reception at the office for our employees, spouses and customers. Then, we gave each employee a check for $410, which was our ranking on the list. The employees all got a kick out of that. It made me think that sometimes it's the little things, like a small token of appreciation for achieving a prestigious goal, that impress people the most. Since I had also dedicated the award that year to my brother John, the celebration was even more satisfying. Later on, we even had several of our employees and their spouses join us on a trip to the award conference, which was held in Miami that year. Not only did we have the chance to kick back and enjoy some time off with our spouses, but it was also an opportunity for these folks to get some recognition too for their role in building our company into something special. Attending conference education sessions, listening to big-name speakers and even just hanging around the pool with all of these other successful entrepreneurs, my guys told me later, was a real inspiration for them.

We have also done some creative things to hand out a few extra bucks from time to time. Starting in 2000, the first year we were profitable,

# Keep *Swinging*

each employee gets 5 percent of his or her salary put into an investment account which is a great recruiting and retention tool. ISI even provided profit sharing in 2003, despite the embezzlement, because it was simply the right thing to do. We also do something for our employees who don't use the company's health insurance plan because they use their spouse's plan instead. I consider a health plan a benefit to each employee, so for those who don't use it, I put the $125 I would pay in premium right back into their paycheck. I just again figured it was the right thing to do.

I also have always believed that another employee retention strategy is that you also need to give your employees the best facilities you can afford. You need to give good people the best tools to do their job with and if you give them some rattletrap office and a slow computer to try to save a few bucks, it will probably be hard to keep them. Quality employees are funny that way. My experience is that they want to work in an environment that is both welcoming and professional. And speaking of skimping, one area no company can afford to be cheap with is in developing their website. Most people nowadays, especially young, tech-savvy folks, will judge the competence of a company based on the professionalism of its website. If you're up for an award or trying to recruit a new employee – or want to brag about your company at a family outing - it's the first place people go to look for information on your company. A good website has become in many ways as important as hiring a good

# Creative Recruiting & Retention

lawyer or banker. That's why we just hired a local company, Visual Thunder, to give us a fresh new look with a logo and website.

At the end of the day, though, you have to promote a level of loyalty among your troops that goes beyond money. We are firmly committed to paying our employees at market levels or above, but there will always be a company willing to pay more, especially for your top performers. And one way to encourage that loyalty is to create a great culture and give your employees a lot of input into the business. One of the advantages of a small business, of course, is that there are usually few levels of management, so everyone's voice and creative ideas can be heard. Based on many years of personal experience you don't get that in a big corporation.

You also don't feel appreciated very often when you work for a big company. People like hearing that they have done a good job and you need to always take time to give positive reinforcement: even if it's just a thank you and a slap on the back. People need to feel appreciated if they are going to stay. And when you treat your people right, they'll treat your customers right and in the end, you will have created an atmosphere of success.

# Keep *Swinging*

A Key Recruit- Derek Plummer and me in 1998. He said he wasn't a risk taker but he moved to join a startup as a newlywed right out of college.

Always Be Recruiting- One of our employees, John DeLockery (VP of Operations) used to be an ISI customer. Here he is at a company seminar in 1999.

# Creative Recruiting & Retention

*Making the INC 500 list in 2001- It's easier to retain employees when they are excited about working for a company that is going somewhere.*

*ISI Does It Again- ISI celebrates at the INC 500 conference in Miami- Treat your employees well and they tend to be loyal to your company for a longer period of time.*

# Keep *Swinging*

2004 ORNL Small Business of the Year- ISI is recognized for "doing what we said we were going to do" on a major A/V video conferencing project.

The 2003 Inaugural Kemmons Wilson Emerging Business Award- A proud moment for ISI since the award was about corporate values, good citizenship and social responsibility.

# Creative Recruiting & Retention

Caption: ISI's 10th Anniversary Party- Celebrating with daughter Katie (far left) Maureen and son Jordan (on right) - Starting and growing ISI, despite all the obstacles and challenges, has exceeded my wildest dreams.

# Chapter Eight

# BACK TO SCHOOL

*Getting more education can be an incredibly profitable experience*

At about the same time that I dissolved my partnership back in 1997, I came to the realization that I had rushed into this business: I was desperate back when I started ISI. I regretted that I never had the luxury of time to think things through, to actually write a real business plan that could help shape not just the next year's forecast, but 10, 15 or even 20 years down the road. That's when I started thinking like a consultant. If I were looking in at this business from the outside, how would I add an extra spark that could take it to the next level?

One of the first things I did after the breakup was to start reaching out to all of my customers and vendors to explain what had happened between my partner and me. I wanted to convince them that I had the financial backing to be in business for a long time. I also made the decision to bring in some new blood – a new engineer and a savvy sales guy to ramp up the revenues coming in the door. But I also wanted to develop a game plan for ISI's future.

So I went searching for ideas in the newspapers – what kinds of innovative strategies are other CEOs in similar situations turning to? That's

# Keep *Swinging*

when I read an article in the Commercial Appeal, the local Memphis newspaper that talked about an upcoming business class that was being offered through the University of Memphis. The class was called Fast Trac and was sponsored by the Ewing Kauffman Foundation, a non-profit organization in Kansas City started by a former business guy of the same name that promotes the interests of small business owners and entrepreneurs like me. A little light bulb popped up in my head – yeah, like me.

While I had always relied on my brother and my dad for good counsel in running my business, I also knew I could use some more education about how to run a successful business. For the record, each of them had started businesses – my dad a weekly newspaper, my brother John an art and framing shop – that each ended up failing. After all, I had actually used a manual typewriter to cobble together the financial projections that I included in my original business plan. Some technology company, huh? I thought FastTrac could give me that edge I was looking for to kick Interactive Solutions into another gear. After learning that the class moderator was slated to be Dr. Barry Gilmore, one of my professors back from my earlier days at the University of Memphis, I decided to enroll.

FastTrac kicked off in the fall of 1998, where I and about a dozen other local entrepreneurs gave up one night every week for three months to talk about a variety of issues including the value of developing a high quality business plan. At the FastTrac class I was discussing topics like

# Back To School

key objectives, marketing budgets, advertising and financial projections with my fellow entrepreneurs, a group that included an auctioneer, a healthcare recruiter and a guy whose company sold manual transmissions. At first, I wondered if I might be in the wrong place: what could I learn from these folks? But, as I stuck it out, I came to realize that Fast Trac was a pleasant surprise. I learned more about how to run a business than I ever would have imagined listening to those other CEOs and their particular challenges – particularly because they were facing different kinds of issues than I was.

One night a guest speaker was talking about how critical a healthy cash flow is to a company's health. That's when the guy with the transmission business spoke up. He talked about how he had recently run into a cash flow crunch of his own and told all of us how he dealt with it. He got all his employees together on a Friday afternoon, he said, looked each one of them in the eye and explained that he was short on cash that week and couldn't make payroll. If you want to walk away, no hard feelings, just business, he said he told them. As he told the story, he paused for dramatic effect. That's when his shop foreman stood up, and said, "If you can give us beer money, we'll hang with you. That got big laughs all around and it's a story I'll never forget. Beyond even the learning opportunity, I loved hanging out with these guys. It felt good connecting with folks that were wired a lot like I was.

# Keep *Swinging*

I finished my class around Christmas time and I couldn't have asked for a better gift – for my business and for me. Not only had I now completed a professional-caliber business plan, I had earned some renewed confidence in where I was headed. The fact that my classmates voted me "most likely to be the next Memphis millionaire" may have also had a thing to do with that. What pleases me even more is the leap that Interactive Solutions took soon afterwards. Sales grew ten-fold, from $1.5 million to more than $10 million in just five years. Needless to say, the success of my company gave me the financial wherewithal to not only pay back my debts in full, but to pay back those that put their trust in me, namely my employees and my family, whether that be a hefty raise or a trip to New York City. For the first time in my life, I didn't have some kind of debt, financial or personal, haunting me.

While the process was an expensive investment in so many ways, both in time and money, making the decision to fire my partner was not only one of the best decisions I ever made for the benefit of my business – it was the best decision I ever made for myself. I was finally independent – with the confidence to do this on my own - and it really propelled me and the company into 1999.

That FastTrac experience also cemented my belief that I would always reach out for new ways to educate myself in how to run my business better, whether that was auditing classes at the University of Memphis or the local community college. While it can be incredibly difficult for a small business owner to justify taking time away from the business to sit in a classroom, that time away from the office can get you out of the weeds for a little while and give you the chance to look back at a problem, get some objective feedback, and think up some creative solutions to use the following day. But going back to school can take many different forms – any of which can be incredibly profitable for an entrepreneur, their company and the people within it. While running my own business, and making all the hard decisions, can be intoxicating, I have to continually remind myself that I don't know it all: not by a long shot. That is why I have continued to invest in my own professional development, in both time and money, by attending seminars hosted by organizations like my bank who re-taught me the importance of cash-flow management and where to look for trouble spots on my financial statements, and the Service Corps of Retired Executives, known as Score. Score is a non-profit organization made up of volunteers most of who ran sizable companies of their own at one time, whose purpose now is to help other entrepreneurs right their own ships. I attended several one-day seminars sponsored by Score on topics like sales and marketing, where I picked up a few tricks. The handful of Inc. 500 conferences I have now attended have also been very helpful, if nothing more than you having a chance to get some feedback from a forum of your fellow entrepreneurs.

# Keep *Swinging*

In a similar vein, I also tapped into a local Memphis group called the Society of Entrepreneurs, where, for the price of a $25 lunch, I continue to get invaluable advice and wisdom from both successful and less than fortunate local entrepreneurs who speak about some of the challenges of growing their businesses. For example, I heard the story of Robert Wang, a local success story who grew his business into a $100-million handicraft-giftware enterprise largely on orders from one customer, and then saw his company collapse after that same customer put the screws to him. The lesson that day was, obviously, spread your risk out by developing more than one customer. I also learned a key lesson from Mike Bruns, who runs Comtrak, an enormously successful trucking company in Memphis, who told us that any good leader should be a part of the team, drinking coffee with his or her crew rather than lording over them from his or her throne. Again, maybe this stuff is obvious to everyone, but to get these kinds of lessons straight from these local legends was priceless to me.

Unexpectedly I even reaped some benefits a few years ago when I took part in a local program called Leadership Collierville, which was an effort to teach people in the community about how the local government works as well as establishing their own role as a leader in the community. I was part of an eclectic group to say the least: the pastor of the Methodist church, a real estate broker and the chief of police were just some of the folks I swapped stories with during the one day a month we

# Back To School

spent together engaged in everything from diversity training to a road trip to the state capital in Nashville to sit in on a state legislature session. While that program certainly gave me a behind-the-scenes peek at how both my local and state government worked, the biggest benefit of the program was with the connection I made with one of my classmates, who just happened to be in charge of purchasing video conferencing equipment for FedEx. Talk about a lucky break: she set up a meeting with me after we graduated from the program and signed an order for more than a $1 million in equipment from ISI. She later told me that it was because she got to know me through this program and not from a random sales call, that she felt she could trust me.

Not only did I take this as a compliment from my friend at FedEx, I now recognize how important it is to connect with local companies and universities. Both businesses and schools alike typically prefer to do business with local companies they can trust. This is especially true when it comes to developing a strong bond with local educational institutions like we do at the University of Memphis. We continue to invest in our relationship with the U of M, one that continues to pay us back time and time again. One of the ways that we do this is through the Myers family memorial scholarship we set up in memory of my parents and brothers that pays the tuition of a student, if he or she maintains at least a B average. As part of the scholarship, the student also spends time working at ISI as an intern, which is both great training for the student

# Keep *Swinging*

and a potential recruiting tool for us. I have also gone back several times to speak to my former professor and mentor Barry Gilmore's undergraduate entrepreneurship class – which is a total blast. "Going back to school" is a tremendous opportunity to work on your presentation skills and present yourself in a leadership role. Based on the thank you letters I have received, the kids truly appreciate the chance to hear frank talk about both the ups and the downs of running your own business. Strangely enough, speaking to these classes has proven to be great therapy for me, where it really felt good to talk about the break up with my partner or with the embezzlement in the context of helping young entrepreneurs avoid making the same mistakes I did. And, rather than scaring off people, these talks have also proven to be great for recruiting: in addition to the thank you letters, I continue to receive an equal number of resumes from young folks from as far away as Austria that would love to come to work for ISI.

And, as a leader, I have always tried to extend the same back-to-school benefits to my employees as well. Either through university classes or similar ones sponsored by organizations like Fred Pryor, ISI has paid for employees to attend classes in everything from organizing remote offices, to managing difficult and emotional employees. Not only do these employees come back from their classes and training with great ideas, it builds goodwill: these employees feel good that the company believes enough in them to invest in their skills, which is such a key part

122

# Back To School

to retaining your best employees. And, as I said earlier, no one can know everything, so the more you invest in educating your employees, as well as yourself, the more profit – both financially and intellectually - everyone can reap from the experience.

A Diploma that Paid Off- ISI Grew from a $1.5M company in 1998 to over $10M in 2004 after I graduated from the Kauffman Foundation FastTrac Class.

# Chapter Nine

# HONESTY, INTEGRITY AND ETHICS
*There is a right way to run a business*

In May 2003, I was truly at a crossroads: I had the option of turning left and letting my employees and the entire Memphis business community know that I had hired a pair of embezzlers, or, I could have easily turned right, and swept the whole Linda and Angela affair under the rug and chalked up the entire experience to just bad luck. In the end, however, there really wasn't any question which direction I was headed. I chose to send those letters to my employees, to come clean with my customers, vendors and even the press because I wanted to show what kind of business we were, the kind of business we still are. I believe that a company's reputation is one of, if not the most valuable asset it has and I wanted to send a strong message by prosecuting Linda that ISI stood for honesty, integrity and ethics in business.

We've all read the stories about companies like WorldCom and Enron, and about how their leaders are now spending their days in jail. I wonder what kind of example folks like Bernie Ebbers and Jeff Skilling set for their employees? Even more importantly, it took folks getting fired before they blew the whistle on the way those companies were cooking their books. How might those situations have come out differently if everyone had been more willing to be up front about their problems?

The high-tech business, unfortunately, is fraught with deception. We run across a lot of competitors who are less than honest with their customers, selling capabilities they don't have or making up a story about why they can't cover a service contract just to make their sales quota or earn an extra buck. I just can't tolerate that kind of behavior and that's why, when it came to making that decision about Linda, I saw an opportunity to make an example out of her, to see that justice was done. Any company that makes a commitment to operating ethically can distinguish itself from its competition. It's just like Superman said, "Truth, justice and the American way". I know that may sound corny, like it's from some by-gone era, and it may just be the Boy Scout in me. But it's how I was raised and it is those values I intend ISI to represent.

## A Family Legacy

The biggest fear I have as the CEO of ISI is that someone will file a complaint with the Better Business Bureau about us. Not only do my family ties run deep with the BBB because of my father and my brother, but I have now been on the board of directors of the Memphis bureau for over

# Honesty, Integrity and Ethics

4 years. From the first days that I launched the business, I remember both my father and brother constantly reminding me that most businesses set out to just make money – it takes an extra effort to do it the right way. My dad told me that starting a business is hard work, but it is only half the job. The other half is running it the right way, knowing that when you put your head on your pillow every night, you know you did the right thing. You don't read that in many books on how to start a business. That's why I used my father's advice to build ISI on the pillars of honesty, integrity, ethics and giving back to the community. Even though he's gone now, I still want to make him proud. And yes, I have even brought several Boy Scout leaders into ISI to help teach our message. But, in always trying to practice what we preach, I have to admit it isn't always easy.

The biggest challenge for me personally is trust. That run-in with Linda and Angela has changed me forever and I'm not sure I will ever be able to trust people the same way again. Because of that, I still call in the payroll every week and deposit 95 percent of the checks. But trust needs to permeate the company from one end to the other and we have run into trouble in finding enough people that share our values. Sure, we run background checks on employees, but, as the Linda story proves, that isn't foolproof by any means. Even though we try to make it clear what we stand for in our employee handbook, which borrows a lot of language about our legal and ethical standards right from the BBB, we still have had problems with other employees as well. For example, we recently hired a guy who had been recommended to us. Well, he left after just a week when he got a better offer somewhere else. We had another employee who was working on the side for one of our competitors. Then there was the sales guy we hired in Birmingham, Alabama, who filed false sales calls reports for an entire year: turns out he hadn't made a single call. Now I know that it's just about impossible to avoid these kinds of things, but this just gets back to how important it is to retain your best and most trustworthy employees, especially because you can't afford to risk the relationships you have with your customers.

I gave a speech about values in early 2007 to a business fraternity at the University of Tennessee in Knoxville. I talked about how when it came to our customers, we never deceived them and never took any short cuts: we give them straight talk backed up with hard work. It is essential to do right by our customers and, at a minimum, that means doing what you say you will do, like delivering products on or ahead of time. Where we have made our mark though, is by taking our commitment to serving our customers to the next level. We have built our brand upon responding to our customers needs not because we had a contract with them but because it was the right thing to do. Is it always easy to do? No, especially when you're in the heat of the battle. Does it sometimes cost

# Honesty, Integrity and Ethics

you a few dollars out of your wallet? You bet. I have on occasion spent thousands of dollars of the company's money to upgrade a customer's software or to send a technician on the road to solve a last-minute problem. And that's also why we continue to make sure we always have a live person answering the phones during business hours – and why my technicians have cell phones for the hours after that. Sure it costs me more to have an operator than a computerized system, but when a customer calls up, there is nothing more comforting that hearing another human voice. Rather than making people punch numbers into their phone in frustration, we let them know that someone has heard their request and that something will be done about it. The customer will get a call back from us, even if it's just to tell them we may not be able to deliver on their request right away. It is a measure of respect and courtesy that I wish I could experience more often when I have to deal with problems with say, my cable TV or Internet service at home. It drives me crazy to have to navigate through some menu, only to leave a voice mail that I know will never be heard. It's a simple thing to answer the phone when a customer is calling, even when you're busy, and I've never regretted making sure everyone else at ISI does the same.

As much as we make that commitment to our customers, we expect the same from them. If we find that a customer doesn't share our values or operate within our standards, we don't want them. We had a customer in Nashville that we found to be unethical and untrustworthy, so we fired them. While that was a difficult decision from the money side, we had to follow our own standards. And sometimes that means not going after customers, even if they are asking you to do business with them. Back when I started ISI, I had to work around a non-compete agreement I signed with ATS that said I wouldn't sell to any business where they sold their telephony products and services – which included many of the colleges and universities where I had previously sold video conferencing products. My lawyer though told me that I could get around it. They can't stop you from going after your customers, he told me. Maybe it was just the fine print, but when I signed that agreement, I made a commitment. So I stuck to that commitment for a year and when it expired, our customers were waiting for us.

Making a commitment to your customers should begin even as you put together your business plan – as part of your operating strategy that doesn't involve making money. It's a philosophy you need to adopt. Customers can buy from anyone and it is up to you to make yourself irresistible to them. Our customers on the whole have praised us for our efforts in working with them – and riding to their rescue from time to time. We killed one of our first clients, PSI, Inc. with kindness. We did more for them in training, configuring equipment and responding to customer service calls not only because we wanted to do the right thing, but also to gain their trust. If we wanted to grow the business, we needed them as a reference.

# Honesty, Integrity and Ethics

But that attitude of going above and beyond the norm becomes contagious. On another occasion, we had a client, Computer Services Inc. in Paducah, Kentucky, call us up in a panic. They had a big training session scheduled for the next day with a few clients of their own, but their system wasn't working properly. I didn't hesitate for a second: I asked two of my guys to hop in the car and make the four-hour drive immediately. And those guys worked literally through the night to fix, test and reassure the CSI folks that their system was operational. My guys even stayed for the session to make sure it went off without a hitch. Again, we didn't have a contract or anything that said we had to do that – it was just the right thing to do. And the examples go on and on, from a law firm where we hooked up three offices in a week to AutoZone in Memphis, where we actually repaired equipment they had bought from another vendor.

And most of the credit for this heroic approach to customer service belongs with my team. We have continually run into situations where my guys have had to work long hours and weekends to make good on a timetable we agreed to. One of my favorite stories involves Don Cottam and Columbia State Community College in Columbia, Tennessee, where we had set up a distance-learning classroom. We got the call one day though that one of the teacher's at the school was out sick and they wondered if anyone from ISI would be willing to teach a class on the technology we used. Don drove up there and proctored the class to help some students. Don didn't have to do it – he too just felt it was the right thing to do to help bail out a customer.

As we were writing this book, ISI was also named as a semi-finalist in yet another award reflective of our values: the Better Business Bureau of Middle Tennessee's Torch Award for Marketplace Ethics. As you can imagine, being recognized for this award – win or lose - was like completing the circle for me in many ways. Not only is the award sponsored by an organization near and dear to my family, it represents everything I have tried to build in my company. Like my dad said, I know that when I put my head on my pillow at night, that I acted as honestly and ethically as I could.

# Chapter Ten

# GIVING BACK

*A business is not only about making money it is about giving back to the community*

In the wake of ISI's recovery following our embezzlement scandal, Maureen came to me with an idea. She reminded me how much ISI and its employees had been through over the prior few years, starting with the partnership divorce and culminating in sending Linda to jail. Maybe, she told me, it was time to take a breath and thank everyone for his or her support. And by everyone, she meant not only the employees, but also the entire community, who through their letters and well wishes encouraged us to always keep our heads up. Maureen's idea was to set up a charity in the company's name called ISI Gives Back that would donate money to any cause suggested by our employees; where each individual in the company could help shape where our donation went. I thought it was genius. While we as a family were involved in our own scholarship programs at both the University of Memphis and Christian Brothers High School, we didn't have any consistency about where the company was involved.

So Maureen got to work setting up the framework for the program, which started with sending out a letter to each of the employees letting them know that we needed their help – we needed their suggestions of who we should be helping outside the walls of ISI. We told them that with all the publicity ISI had received for its success, we were contacted all the time by organizations looking for money. Rather than giving money to people we didn't already have a connection with, we asked for our employee's help in telling us where we could best give back - who were the people in the community that we could help or give thanks to?

Our employees responded to our letter with great enthusiasm and, to no one's surprise, the program was a big hit with everyone involved. We not only helped churches in the community, but severely under-funded schools as well. In particular, we bought flash cards and picture dictionaries for an inner-city program run by the wife of one of our employees and donated a bunch of audio-visual equipment to another elementary school where the kids got the chance to learn how to use some cutting-edge educational tools.

Maureen's idea for a giveback program was an important reminder to me that in order to be a good company, you also need to be a good corporate citizen. It is not an option – it is an obligation. Not only does this help foster a sense of honesty and integrity in the business, but people in the community recognize that level of involvement as well. People want to do business with companies that contribute to the community as a whole. In other words, giving back simply makes for good business

# Giving Back

in so many ways, from networking with other community and business leaders to recruiting and retaining our employees. If we aren't able to promote balance in the goals of our company, we will have failed our obligation to give something back. That's why we do everything we can to support the Memphis Redbirds and its RBI program: a volunteer-led effort whose goal is to return baseball to the inner city and encourage more minorities to play America's pastime. With my own personal love of baseball, supporting the program promotes positive social change and has been deeply rewarding. We also support an outdoor concert series hosted by the local botanical garden, a non-profit organization that promotes green space and conservation in and around the Memphis area. Each summer, we buy tickets to shows like Sheryl Crow and Michael McDonald for all of our employees and their families to attend. We get the good seats too so that our employees and customers get the real VIP treatment. Who said that giving back to the community can't be a whole lot of fun?

And giving back doesn't just involve donating equipment and money – it can be even more valuable to give your time. Picture this: you walk into a classroom not unlike one that you used to sit in as a 10 year old. It's early, 8:00 a.m., when that bell sounds off, which helps wake you up when you're too young for coffee. Remember the chalkboards, the desks (that now seem so small) and even the cubbyholes where you used to stash your jacket, boot and book bag. Now fill those little desks with 22

# Keep *Swinging*

wide-eyed boys and girls; boys dressed in green polo shirts and tan slacks, girls in plaid dresses. Now, as you walk to the front of the room accompanied by a teacher, Mrs. Drane in this case, all eyes focus on you. While you may be the father of two, and the CEO of a company, nothing quite prepares you for this. It's Junior Achievement day, and you're at that class to teach those young folks about business basics. "Hello Mr. Myers," they say in unison. Talk about nerve wracking! I have a renewed respect for what teachers like Mrs. Drane do (and I say that even before I realized that she was St. Louis Cardinal's shortstop and 2006 World Series MVP David Eckstein's mother-in-law.)

I have actually been an instructor with Junior Achievement for about 17 years, a national non-profit program that teach some 7 million kids about the basics of business and entrepreneurship like balancing a checkbook or making a bank deposit. The former president of JA, in fact, was the one who introduced me to ISI's initial funder – so I feel a deep sense of obligation to repaying that debt. What I discovered along the way though is that there is a real fulfillment in educating children, even if it is just for a few hours a year, especially when you feel as if you helped them connect with something of importance in themselves. I have had young adults stop me on several occasions in places like the grocery store, letting me know they still appreciated the things I taught to them years earlier in those classes.

# Giving Back

And there are real benefits to be earned through programs like Junior Achievement, especially in low-income areas like Memphis. In my time with JA, both as an instructor and more recently as a board member, I've come to call Ray Darby, the president of the Memphis and Mid-South chapter of JA, a friend. Ray also happens to be a neighbor of mine in Collierville. I went down to visit Ray one day at JA's downtown headquarters, a fantastic location built five years ago whose 20,000 square foot ground floor is devoted to Exchange City, a mock main street of sorts that allows JA students to run their own business for a day. Ray told me that JA's main goals are to help end disturbing trends like Memphis's high unemployment rate, which is 40 percent higher than the national average, or that 40 percent of the Memphis community has no relationship with a banking institution of any kind. "That why you see those long lines at the Piggly Wiggly every weekend," Ray told me. "Folks are cashing their checks and then using the cash to pay off their utility bills at the stalls set up in there. Many of the parents of the kids in our program don't even know how to fill out a check at all anyway."

That's why the JA curriculum I teach my 22 fifth-graders involves teaching them everything from managing a checking account to how to look, act and dress up for a job interview. And while I don't hit them with full guns blazing, I don't dumb down the subject matter as I explain how I started ISI or when we role play situations like how to get the most bang for your buck in an advertising campaign or the challenges in mass producing a product. These kids are bright and it's amazing how quickly they can grasp complex subjects when given the right opportunity. The key is to coach them, but let them run with it, to learn by doing. And that's the real promise behind Exchange City. Just about every school day, one lucky class shows up at this pillar of commerce to buy goods and services from each other, lend money and even hand out traffic fines if you are the one lucky student elected judge. The students earn salaries for their jobs, bank officers earn more than the snack counter folks do, and the kid's shave to interview for the jobs beforehand to earn their spot in the prime jobs (I hope the interview skills I taught my class served them well). And by earning real money, and learning how to both save and spend it, these kids are learning essential skills not only for the business world, but also for living their lives as well. Hopefully, these kids then go home and teach their brothers and sisters, maybe even their parents, about everything they learned.

Matter of fact, JA has partnered with the RISE Foundation (Responsibility, Initiative, Solutions and Empowerment), a local organization that advocates for financial literacy in adults, to develop a certification program to help connect employers with graduates from the joint JA-RISE program. Hopefully we are helping to build the next generation of entrepreneurs who will, at the very least, think they can achieve great things. As my friend and mentor Kemmons Wilson was known to say, "There are two ways to get to the top of an oak tree: one way is to sit on an acorn and wait; the other way is to climb it."

# Giving Back

I have had such a blast being involved with JA that I have encouraged folks on my management team at ISI like Linda Godsey, John DeLockery, Julia Chrestman, Joan Blanton and Annelle Hochhauser to get involved as well. And so that they don't run into conflicts with their families, I pay them to go on company time. The unexpected benefit of this has been the spirit of camaraderie this has promoted with us, as we share tips and lesson plans to help each other prepare to teach. Working towards a common goal has been a great team building exercise for us and, I hope, really cemented some notion about being a part of something more than just making money.

## Scouts Honor

If I could point to any one organization that I have modeled the values of ISI upon besides the BBB it would be the Boy Scouts, something I have been a part of my entire life. I am an Eagle Scout as also is my son Jordan. I have personally served as a merit badge counselor in business and salesmanship and have been on numerous boards of review, where I had the priceless opportunity to have a positive impact on a young man's life. John DeLockery has also been very involved with Scouting and his 2 sons are also Eagle scouts. In fact it was John that recommended that ISI could help out a Scout in need by using our technology to assist one young man in passing his Eagle Scout board of review: The young man had recently relocated from Memphis to Denver (for his father's job) after the sudden death of his mother. He had one final step to complete his Eagle Scout award which was to pass his board of review with the local Scout leaders from Memphis. When the time came, ISI was proud to donate some time and equipment to connect the scout up via video conference and help him earn the award. It is moments like that that make me proud to own a technology business that not only makes money but has the ability to improve people's lives.

Being a part of the Boy Scouts is the best leadership training program in the world and when I see Eagle Scout listed on someone's resume - that is a real eye opener for me. A scout, above all, is a man with integrity and that symbolizes everything I believe in both in life and business. A proud moment for me was when I was recently awarded the Silver Beaver Award, the highest award an adult can earn from the scouts for distinguished service to young people in their community. For someone that had been involved in scouting for over 15 years as a young man and adult, it doesn't get any better than that. One key lesson I have learned from the scouts and other community volunteer work I have done – and I have applied to my life at home and in the office – is that when you do good, good things happen to you.

# Giving Back

*ISI and Junior Achievement - Jay Myers teaching the JA Business Basics class at Incarnation Catholic School.*

*Eagle Scout Board of Review Goes High Tech-ISI uses video conferencing to help a Boy Scout in Denver qualify for his Eagle Scout Award in Memphis.*

# Keep *Swinging*

*Everybody gets into the Act - Julia Chrestman, Administrative Assistant, presenting diplomas at the end of a JA class at an inner city school.*

# AFTERWORD: KEEP SWINGING

While I might have dreamed of owning my own business for a long time, I've fantasized about donning the pinstriped uniform of the New York Yankees since I was five years old. Little did I know that by fulfilling one of those pipedreams that would make the other one come true as well.

First off, how could I, a lifelong southerner, you might ask, grow up as a Yankees fan? Well, they were my dad's favorite team: he grew up in Oklahoma, near Mickey Mantle's hometown. I still vividly remember the first baseball bat my dad gave me in 1961 – a plastic model engraved with the names of Mickey Mantle and Roger Maris that commemorated their historic run at Babe Ruth's homerun record that year. And that link was further cemented a few years later when our family moved to Memphis and I, as a 4th grade Little Leaguer, got drafted by the Germantown Yankees. I even got to wear the no. 7 on my jersey, and my connection to Mantle and the Yankees was complete.

I will say that it wasn't easy to wear pinstripes in St. Louis Cardinals country in the 1960s. Memphis, of course, has been the longtime home of the Cardinal's farm team, the Redbirds. I even had a friend I played with in 7th grade who was the nephew of Tim McCarver, the Cardinal's

# Keep *Swinging*

great catcher and now TV announcer. He used to get on me all the time about rooting for the Yankees: especially after the Cardinals outlasted them in seven games to win the 1964 World Series. While I was a fair to above-average player myself, I was destined for glory smacking slow-pitch softballs, not patrolling centerfield in New York City. I always kept up my love for the game, though, even through college where I joined all my classmates on a trip to Fort Lauderdale, Florida, where the Yankees' played their spring training games each spring. While most of my buddies headed to the beach, I always made time to catch a few games and hang around afterwards to get the autographs of the greats at that time like Thurman Munson, Catfish Hunter and even Reggie Jackson, who I once waited two hours for before he showed up to sign one of my baseballs. Two of my favorite moments watching the team live have been, first, in March of 1982, when Maureen and I went to watch the Yankees play an exhibition game against the Texas Rangers in the Louisiana Super Dome, and in September 2001, when I made the first of what I hope will be many pilgrimages to the hallowed ground of Yankee Stadium in the Bronx. From our amazing seats we got to watch the Yankees beat up on their archrivals, the Boston Red Sox. I don't know what heaven is like, but that had to be close to it.

Well, if I hadn't clued you in to this already, Maureen has a pretty keen eye for detail and she knew how much the Yankees mean to me. That's why she handed me a very special envelope one night at dinner during

# Afterword

a family vacation in the summer of 2006. "What's this," I asked. "Your 50th birthday present," she said, with a big smile. "I thought you deserved to get it a bit early." As I opened that envelope, I just about fell out of my chair: inside was in invitation to attend the Yankees Fantasy Camp that coming January. As excited as I was about fulfilling the dream of putting on a real Yankees uniform, I was just as determined not to make a fool out of myself. I hadn't fielded a grounder let alone swung a bat in quite some time and, as I approached that magic age of 50, I knew I needed to boost my training regimen. I started working out with Larry Robinson, a strength coach who also played with the Milwaukee Brewers at one time. We spent countless hours taking batting practice, trying to recapture some of my old skills from 30 years ago. I even took the field with the team from my old high school, Christian Brothers, to gain some confidence during some game action. Despite all the work in the gym and on the field, I still wondered if I would be ready when I finally heard those magic words, "play ball."

When January 15, 2007, finally rolled around, and I headed down to Tampa, my childhood fantasy began to come true. I was joined by an odd collection of fans as nuts as I was, like a guy who drove a truck for DHL and an exec from the Discovery Channel. We had folks from all walks of life. The only requirement of coming was that you needed to be older than 30. There was no upper age limit, and I'll tell you what: our catcher was an 83-year-old guy named Gus, and I hope I'll be out on the diamond at that age myself. On that first night, we had a meet-and-greet cocktail party with the coaches and other players, where we got to ask all-time Yankee greats like Tom Tresh, Tommy John, Mickey Rivers, Mel Stottlemyre, Oscar Gamble, Paul Blair, Ken Griffey and Al Downing to autograph jerseys and baseballs. I can't begin to describe what a thrill it was.

As fun as it was to meet these guys, what we came here to do was play some ball. And, in a pinstriped uniform of my own, we played 18 innings or two games each and every day. I remember trotting out to left field for the first time, the freshly cut, green grass spongy beneath my feet, the Florida sun warm on my back where I proudly wore the no. 7 in tribute to my childhood hero Mickey Mantle. As I turned to face home plate, crouched, my hands on my bent knees, I was transported back in time: I was 12 again, roaming left field for my middle school squad back in Memphis. I remember sweating after all those two-a-day practices, countless hours of batting practice and shagging flyballs as the sun set until, finally, one day it was time for the games to count for real. And as I blinked myself back to real time again, all the pain and angst I'd bottled up over the past few years melted away. I smiled and waited for the pitcher to wind up, to hear the crack of the bat hoping, just maybe, the batter would hit the ball to me.

# Afterword

I know that each of the guys on the field with me felt something similar: here we were, getting a chance to relive our youth. How many people can say that? And we had a blast – because of our different ages and backgrounds, we had a good mix of skilled players, including a couple of ringers that could really smoke the ball. Fortunately, because of all the hard work I did with Larry, I more than held my own: I went 10 for 22, good, for a Joe Dimaggio-esque average of .455, including a key RBI double. That bit of confidence helped as we moved into the last day, a Saturday, to play a final two-inning game against a lineup of the legends: with no less than Tommy John on the mound. And my teammates and I couldn't have been more excited to play that wrap-up game: not only was it a chance to take the field against some of our heroes, it also meant we might finally get some rest when it was done! While baseball looks like an easy game, playing 72 innings of baseball over four days took its toll – we were all in various states of pain. It really gave me a renewed respect for the professionals who play basically every day for six straight months.

Despite our various aches and pains, many of my new friends and I had tears in our eyes as we huddled up before we took the field: we were truly fulfilling a dream by taking the field to play against the idols from our childhoods. As we took the field, the butterflies in my stomach were jumping – but nothing like when I dug into the batter's box to face off against a man who won 288 games in pitching for 26 years in the big leagues. It was a special moment, even surreal. As Bob Sheppard, the legendary Yankee Stadium announcer, called out my name, a huge picture of me flashed up on the outfield scoreboard, and old Tommy threw me a strike right down the pipe. I gave it a good poke to the left side of the infield. As third-baseman Jim Leyritz, who starred in two World Series, made a diving stop, popped up and gunned the ball over to first, I hustled, hitting the bag just before the ball popped into Mickey Rivers glove. SAFE!

I share this story because I could not have made this dream come true without the help of a lot of people. Obviously, I need to thank Maureen for my gift, but I need to thank everyone else as well who made ISI into what it has become, because if not for the success of the company none of this would have been possible. That is the cool feeling about entrepreneurship – not only did I get to take control of my life, I got to live out a fantasy because of it. That's a lesson I hope anyone can learn from: no matter how tough things got, I just kept swinging. While the results may not always have been pretty, I am proud of every one of them.

# Afterword

*Living out my baseball fantasy-January 2007*

# ACKNOWLEDGEMENTS

My heartfelt thanks go out to all the people who helped make this book a reality. I'd like to thank my publisher, David Hancock, and all the folks at Morgan James Publishing who believed in our project from the beginning. Thank you to Ann Crawford, our author relations manager at Morgan James, and Margo Toulouse who have patiently dealt with all of our crazy problems and requests and kept us on track.

I would also like to thank all of our friends at Inc. magazine for your long-time support and for playing such an important role in the development of ISI.

At Junior Achievement I would like to thank Ray Darby, Larry Colbert, Jennifer Loving and the entire staff and board of directors who have provided such great support and allowed us to tell the ISI/JA story.

I also want to thank all the volunteers and staff of the Chickasaw Council of the Boy Scouts of America for allowing us to be a part of the finest youth organization in the world.

# Keep *Swinging*

Thanks also to James Overstreet, Mark Watson, David Flaum and all the folks at the Memphis Commercial Appeal for their phenomenal newspaper coverage of ISI for the last several years.

Many thanks also to all the folks at the Memphis Business Journal who were early believers in ISI and have continued to provide such strong support and encouragement since we started in 1996.

I would also like to thank all the people at the Kauffman Foundation for their continued support of the FastTrac program that has been such an integral part of ISI's success.

I would like to thank Drs. Shirley Raines, John Pepin, Barry Gilmore and all of our friends at the University of Memphis who have been loyal ISI supporters from the beginning.

I would like to thank the entire staff and board of directors of the Better Business Bureau of the Mid South and Middle Tennessee whose commitment to marketplace ethics and integrity have made ISI a better company.

And lastly many thanks to my assistant, Julia Chrestman who helped me put all of this together- You have the patience of a saint!

## Bonus Section

# "BE ONE OF THE SURVIVORS"

Don't be in the 96% of the Small Businesses

that don't make it to 10 years.

Be in the 4% that do!!!

Have you checked your business plan lately?

## MAYBE YOU SHOULD!

Let me offer you this bonus DVD download valued at over $250 that will give you some "Special Survival Tips" your business plan probably doesn't include but could put you and your company right on the TOP in the 4% with the

## SURVIVORS

**Visit:  keepswingingbook.com/bonus**

**Password: OutofthePark07**

# ABOUT THE AUTHORS

## JAY MYERS

My company, which I founded along with a partner in 1996, is currently based in Memphis, Tennessee. We specialize in selling video conferencing, distance learning, telemedicine and audio-visual equipment and support. Starting from scratch, I, with the help of many others, have built what is now a $14 million company with 40 employees working in offices in Memphis, Nashville, Knoxville Tenn., Birmingham, Ala. and Jackson, Miss.

Our company has received numerous corporate awards and recognition over the past several years including: the Oak Ridge National Labs 2004

# Keep *Swinging*

Small Business of the Year, the 2003 Kemmons Wilson Emerging Business Award from the Memphis Regional Chamber of Commerce and the Memphis Business Journal Small Business of the Year in 2001. Interactive Solutions also earned a spot on both the 2001 and 2003 Inc. 500, the list of fastest growing private companies in the United States.

Prior to starting my company, I worked for ATS Telephone and Data Systems, Inc., as well as Eastman Kodak and Hewlett Packard where I earned numerous sales awards.

I have lived in Memphis since 1965. I graduated from Christian Brothers High School in 1974, and later, in 1978, the University of Memphis. I continue to be involved in numerous local community organizations including the Town of Collierville Mayor's Advisory Board and am an active board member of the Boy Scouts (Chickasaw Council) Junior Achievement of Greater Memphis and the Mid South Better Business Bureau.

I live in Collierville, Tennessee, with my wife Maureen, two children, Jordan and Kaitlin, and our two black Labrador Retrievers, Chuck and Casey.

# About the Authors

## DARREN DAHL

Darren Dahl, a freelance writer and author who I asked to help me write my story, was most recently a staff writer at Inc. magazine in New York City. Prior to joining Inc., Darren earned his Master of Science degree in journalism from Columbia University in New York City. He also holds a Master of Business Administration degree from the State University of New York, Albany and a Bachelor's degree from Union College in Schenectady, New York, where he studied English and economics and graduated with honors. Darren lives with his wife, Jess McCuan, in New York City.

Printed in the United States
122231LV00002B/13-60/P